Yosemite Epics

Tales of Adventure from America's Greatest Playground

To Jeff,

Good climbing!

Yosemite Epics

Tales of Adventure from America's Greatest Playground

Matt Johanson

Matt Johanson

Illustrated by Christopher Hampson

ISBN 978-0-615-39182-3

Editors: William Gracie and Ben Topkins
Photography: Matt Johanson (unless otherwise credited)
Front cover photo: Galen Rowell
Back cover illustration: Christopher Hampson
Cover design, interior design and photo editing: Morry Anne Angell
Web site designer: Jeff Stevens

Printed in the United States

Climbing route lines on photos in this book are approximations and should not be used for trip planning.

Dreamcatcher Publishing
20133 Butterfield Drive
Castro Valley, California 94546
www.dreamcatcherpublishing.com

Library of Congress Control Number 2010933773

For Dad, who taught me to love the outdoors,
and for Mom, who always packed the lunches with love

Contents

Foreword by John Moynier.. 11

Steve Roper: "A Schizophrenic Rock"................................. 15

Howard Weamer and Lynn MacMichael: "A Hard Go"............... 21

Dale Bard: "In the Dead of Winter"................................. 29

Marty McDonnell: "Dance with the Dragon"................................. 37

Errett Allen: "Nature's Power"................................. 45

John Bachar: "I Got Away with One"................................. 57

Royal Robbins: "The Best Medicine"................................. 65

Lynn Hill: "Climbing Wisdom"................................. 71

Hans Florine: "Sandbag Situation"................................. 77

Doug Englekirk: "The Lord Watches Over Me"................................. 85

Steve Schneider: "If God had Meant for Man to Fly"................................. 93

Scott Cosgrove: "Affliction"................................. 99

Peter Croft: "Hunted".. 107

Peter Mayfield: "The Deeper Connection"....................... 113

George Durkee: "Sin and Redemption"............................ 119

Chandlee Harrell: "Surprises"... 125

Majka Burhardt: "Epic Desire".. 131

Noah Kaufman: "Miracle".. 137

Jim Zellers: "The Half-a-Brain Project"........................... 145

Ammon McNeely: "Marooned on a Sea of Granite".................. 151

Richard Leversee and John Wason: "The Nature of an Epic"......... 159

Andy Padlo: "Summit Fever"... 167

Tommy Caldwell: "That Old-School Style"..................... 177

Afterword.. 183

Acknowledgments.. 187

Explanation of Climbing Ratings..................................... 189

Glossary.. 191

Bibliography.. 197

About the Author and Illustrator..................................... 199

Yosemite Valley

Foreword by John Moynier

Dramatic stories of epic Yosemite adventures have been a staple of campfire conversations and must-read compilations since the days of Clarence King and John Muir. We still hunger for them today. Although at first glance Yosemite and the High Sierra may not seem a likely setting for gripping mountain tales, Muir's "Range of Light" does have its dark side. The Sierra may generally be more Disney than Denali, but as these writers have proven, the "Gentle Wilderness" can become decidedly hostile in a hurry, especially when we leave the safety of the lush Valley floor and enter the unforgiving environment found on the sheer granite walls of the vertical world.

But it takes more than a battle with nature to make a compelling epic. We need to connect to heroes, and these writers definitely fill the bill. They represent the best and the brightest of our sport and the list of contributors reads like a "Who's Who" of Yosemite climbing over the past 50 years. These are some of the most accomplished mountaineers of our time. Reading their accounts, we realize that even our heroes can get themselves into bad spots. Through their stories, we vicariously share their suffering, anxiety, hope for survival and sense of accomplishment when they pull through.

It's basic human nature that we enjoy the palm sweats that go with a good epic. Better them than us, I guess. That's especially true if we've had a close call of our own and know something of fear, exhaustion, cold, hunger and the redemptive power of a sunrise or a friendly voice. No one starts out on an adventure hoping to end up in an epic. Yet some adventures do become more than we bargained for. Epic stories provide a safe kind of voyeurism. In these tales, we know that things end okay. While the central characters may get into serious trouble, they must find a way out of it or we'd never hear the tale.

In "The Lord of the Rings," one of grandest (fictional) epic tales of all time, author J.R.R. Tolkien expressed thoughts on this subject as his protagonists found themselves in a rough place.

"We shouldn't be here at all, if we'd known more about it before we started," said Sam. "But I suppose it's often that way…I wonder what sort of tale we've fallen into?"

"I wonder," said Frodo. "But I don't know. And that's the way of a real tale. Take any one that you're fond of. You may know, or guess, what kind of tale it is, happy-ending or sad-ending, but the people in it don't know. And you don't want them to."

That's the way of these stories, too. I hope you enjoy them!

John Moynier is a longtime Sierra Nevada climber, skier and guidebook author.

Steve Roper:
"A Schizophrenic Rock"

As a climber, Steve Roper achieved first ascents including El Capitan's West Buttress and the first one-day climb of Half Dome's Northwest Face. As a writer, he has authored more than a dozen books about his beloved Sierra Nevada, including the first-ever Yosemite climbing guide in 1964 and his award-winning "Camp 4: Recollections of a Yosemite Rockclimber." Countless enthusiasts have benefitted from Roper's matchless body of work combining his two great passions, though warning fellow climbers about the hazards of a death-defying route he helped pioneer may rate among his kindest contributions to the outdoors community.

Middle Cathedral Rock boasts some of the park's greatest routes, such as its moderate and ultra-popular East Buttress. Some of Yosemite's nastiest climbing stands here, too, like the perilous and rarely-climbed North Face. Roper, 18, and partners Bob Kamps and Chuck Pratt had little idea what awaited them when they set out to scale 20 pitches on the dark and cold wall in June of 1959. Before they were finished, however, the trio learned more than they ever wanted to know about loose flakes and dirty, wet rock.

I've always had a love affair with Middle Cathedral Rock. When people stand in the meadow down below it, most of them are looking at El Capitan. I turn around and look at Middle Cathedral, an incredibly beautiful and complex rock and so completely different than El Cap. The flakes are so pretty, the rock the colors of gold and rust. I climbed to the top of this 2,000-foot monolith 17 times by nine different routes, like the East Buttress, the North Buttress, the Direct North Buttress and the Kor-Beck route.

In 1959, the North Face of Middle Cathedral Rock was the biggest unclimbed wall in Yosemite. Half Dome had been done in '57, El Cap in '58. We were looking around for other big walls. My friend Bob Kamps found this wall and we drove down there to take a look at it. Chuck Pratt and I were horrified. We didn't really see a route. The North Face line is not obvious. It looked rotten and bushy. I was only 18 and not terribly experienced. I had bivouacked only once in my life, a month before. But Pratt and Kamps were more experienced and older. Kamps said it would be no problem and he persuaded us. So we started up one day in June.

We took heavy packs, three ropes, climbing shoes with lug soles and about 70 pitons, terrible equipment by today's standards. On the lower part, we climbed 600 feet of low-angle rock using a lot of aid. When we got up to where the wall gets steep, we started to get into some really decomposed rock and hard climbing. We didn't realize beforehand that because the North Face gets so little sun, there would be lots of bad rock, wet cracks and loose flakes hanging like guillotines over chimneys. Water doesn't drain, little bushes grow and lots of things fall down the face of the rock. We had no helmets, though we should have.

I led about five pitches and I remember being quite scared and intimidated by the thing. Then night fell and we came to this little ledge about six feet long and maybe 15 inches wide. We sat there like three morons on a park bench all night long. We had poor equipment, no sleeping bags, no headlamps and certainly no portaledge. It was uncomfortable but we couldn't lie down, so we just sat there with our legs dangling over the side, freezing our asses off. Needless to say, we got little sleep that night.

In the morning, we were faced with just a horrible section of rock. Kamps led on aid and it seemed to take forever. He must have taken two or three hours to get up 100 feet. We couldn't see him from around the corner, but debris rained down on us, chunks of granite and little pieces of bushes and grit. Pratt and I were freezing but we could tell the climbing was hard and nerve-wracking by the sound of the pitons. Instead of ringing with a "ping, ping, ping," they made a sound more like "thunk, thunk, thunk" which comes from rotten rock. A lot of the pitons went behind expanding flakes, so the protec-

North Face of Middle Cathedral Rock   Photo: Dan Johanson

tion was poor. By this time I was scared. I had been doing my share
of the leading down below, so I thought to myself, "I'll let these guys
take over for a while."

Pratt led the next pitch, which was a terrifying chimney, flared,
rotten, very steep and maybe 100 feet long. There was no place to get
in good protection. We had a bolt kit but we didn't stop to place any
bolts. It took a couple of hours to do that hard pitch. When Royal
Robbins did the second ascent later that year, he called Pratt's lead
one of the finest ever done in American climbing.

A couple of pitches above there, I started leading again. Luckily we got up to a huge ledge, so we could stretch out on the second night, though it was still very cold. Down jackets were our only
bivvy gear. We took candy and dates, cans of tuna and about a quart
and a half of water per man per day. Our water ran out on the third
day, but we topped out at about noon and a couple of people hiked
up to meet us with big canteens and some nice food for us. Descending down the back side involved some horrible bushwhacking and
talus, but we got to Camp 4 by about three in the afternoon. And so
that was that, the first ascent of the great Middle Cathedral's North

Face.

You worry about a climb like this beforehand and you don't get any sleep the night before, so it's always a relief to finish it. There's a lot pride when you get a first ascent. You come back to camp with bragging rights. People crowd around you and ask what it was like. You lie a little bit, of course: "It may never be done again!"

The North Face is unpopular and I think it's hardly ever climbed. One of these days, someone may do it again and claim a first ascent! Anyone who does it will have quite an adventure. It won't be like El Cap where modern guidebooks show every single gear placement in advance. Middle Cathedral is a schizophrenic rock and the North Face is not your normal Yosemite climb. This was one of those "this had to be done" type of things. It was beckoning to us.

The main lessons were to prepare for the unknown, avoid decomposed rock and climb with good partners, so they can drag me up if need be. I was good at aid climbing but never a terribly good free climber; I didn't want to fall. I don't ever want to go on such a rotten and ugly climb again but every day on the rock can't be wonderful and sunny. Occasionally you have to have these not-terribly-fun experiences if you want to be a well-rounded climber.

Howard Weamer and Lynn MacMichael: "A Hard Go"

Skiers who have taken shelter in Yosemite's rustic and beautiful Ostrander Hut owe a debt of gratitude to Howard Weamer. More than a few would never have reached the cabin without assistance from Ostrander's caretaker since 1974. Winter adventurers should also thank Lynn MacMichael, a college professor and Weamer's wife who has shared her husband with the backcountry for decades and occasionally helped him rescue lost and weary skiers.

Together the pair attempted a 35-mile trans-Sierra crossing in March of 1979. Weamer, 35, had made the journey several times before while MacMichael, 40, attempted the trek for the first time. An unexpected heavy storm challenged even the godparents of the Yosemite skiing community, teaching the not-yet-married couple a lesson that helped shape their lifetime together.

HW: This was my sixth crossing on the southern border of Yosemite and I had high confidence that things would go well. So right off the bat, I'm traveling without map or compass, basically by line of sight. That's the way I traveled then and that's the way I still travel. I don't have a GPS and I don't even know how to use one. When you're out there in terrain, you're following very large drainage systems and ridges. It's not too hard to figure that out. For this particular trip from Ostrander, go up Horse Ridge and you can see Fernandez Pass. From Fernandez Pass you can see Timber Knob, and so on. That's the route that we took toward Mammoth.

LM: I had spent time at the hut and we had done a couple of trips around Merced Lake and out into the Clark Range, but not a trans-Sierra before. Our longest trip until then was three nights. I wouldn't say I was a skilled skier but I loved being out there. Howard said it would be a cinch.

HW: We made really good time at first. I was surprised that we got past Moraine Mountain and underneath Fernandez on the first night. Then we spotted Timber Knob and crossed a saddle to the north above Cora Lakes. The second night we stopped on a really nice spot above Cora Creek. The next morning we went down to the North Fork of the San Joaquin and found an ice bridge to cross. So we were really rolling along, covering great ground.

At the beginning, we got a forecast for nine days of fair weather from the park service. But by midday of the third day, a storm had come in. The Ritter Range and Mammoth are areas of intense snowfall because storms come up the San Joaquin from the Central Valley and just slam into Iron Mountain and Mammoth. We were just rounding Iron Mountain at the very bottom of the Ritter Range when this thing started to really crank up. Snow fell very heavily and visibility disappeared.

LM: Howard knows the mountains like the back of his hand so I had no idea there would even be a need for a compass, but the storm was really intense. The first clue I got that we needed one was the day the storm came in. We couldn't see 20 feet. We tried to climb up to where we could see where we were going. We were climbing for a long time when we looked down and saw tracks below us. "Great, there are other people here!" I said. And then it dawned on us that the other people were us, and we had simply wasted all that time going around in a circle. Whoops! That was when we knew that first, we were lost, and second, that we didn't really know how to get out of there.

HW: Snow fell all night and all the next day. We traveled the whole day in a snowstorm in the forest. I was happily breaking trail with plastic-based skis, Fischer 77s. Lynn still had her wood skis, and when you skied in the spring, the coatings on the bases would get worn off. When water got absorbed into their wooden bases, snow locked onto them and they became almost impossible to move.

LM: I would get these huge piles of snow under the skis. It made me feel like I was on high heels, like I could break an ankle. I'd have to keep stopping every two minutes to try to shake it off, and then I'd do two more steps and I'd be up there again. It became tricky because I was so unbalanced on this huge ridge of snow.

HW: After we set up our tent near Iron Mountain, there was a break in the clouds that night. I could spot the moon and from that I got a good idea of where our line should go. As we got further and further east the next day, I could see the landscape start to fall away. That's what it was supposed to do on our way to Reds Meadow, which is on the Middle Fork of the San Joaquin River, the next major drop. Well, I took off too early, and we ended up dropping and dropping much too far. The snow got wetter and wetter. We ended up on these rock ledges at the snow line. Obviously we were way too low in elevation. The only thing we could see underneath the clouds was rock bench after rock bench. We ended up making camp on this little bench, just sopping wet with water running everywhere.

LM: The snow was so wet that the night we camped down in the river canyon, we had to keep getting out of the tent to get the snow off it. Otherwise it might have collapsed and we could have suffocated. The tent got absolutely swamped. I remember feeling soaked in the clothes we had, and sleeping with plastic bags over my socks, because everything was wet already and I thought the plastic would at least hold the warmth in.

HW: This is '79 and the foul weather gear eventually gets soaked through. We've got wool pants and wool stays warm even when it's wet. But it was wet and I mean wet! The pants, the socks, the underlayers, the tent, everything. We didn't have the stuff that wicks moisture away like you can get today, and our down sleeping bags weren't providing us with that much warmth.
    We broke that camp on the ledge and started climbing back

up out of the Middle Fork. One of the first things we hit was a manzanita field covered in wet snow. We couldn't ski above it and we couldn't go beneath it. We ended up literally throwing our skis over the manzanita to get through. It was hard work though still basically fun for me.

LM: That manzanita went on forever. You had to throw your pack over the top of the manzanita, covered with ice and snow, and then crawl over that to get your pack again. There was no opening and no other way through it. We kept getting our pants cut up and torn. We were always gaining two feet and losing one. It was very frustrating. I don't think anybody, even Howard, would say that part was fun.

We were climbing up out of the San Joaquin in wind and storm that were just crazy. I could only see the back of him. He wanted to get up high in case there was a break in the storm so we could see where we were. It felt like we climbed 4,000 feet.

As I was passing a pine cone covered with ice and snow that shimmered in the little light there was, I remember thinking this was as good a place to die as any, because it was very beautiful. It wasn't a jail cell or a hospital room with tubes. "Well, if I go, it's a nice place and that's good," I thought.

HW: The storm never came close to breaking that day and a couple of feet of solid snow fell. We didn't have skins at the time so we used rope climbers, these hideous things made out of clothesline which you tied onto the skis for traction. We did eventually work our way up and up and up, maybe a couple of thousand feet. We made camp on this little flat spot.

LM: By this time the rations were getting very small. I really trusted that this was going to be a five day trip and that's the amount of food we took. But we didn't know when the storm would end and didn't think anybody knew where we were. We were down to a handful of granola twice per day.

HW: Sleeping that night, Lynn was hypothermic and shaking. But the next morning, the clouds parted. Lynn said, "Get out, get out quick, we'll see something!" I bolted out of the tent and through a little opening of the clouds, I could see Minaret Summit. This little hole in the sky didn't last more than 20 seconds, but I knew where I was. From there, I saw a ridge that climbed up towards Mammoth Mountain. Then I spotted two other knobs in the Middle Fork canyon which guided us to Reds Meadow. So we packed up to go.

I skied out to the lip and jumped on the edge a little bit, and kicked down a crown avalanche. So I thought, okay, we're obviously not going to ski down this steep open slope. But fortunately, there was a ridge edge with a few trees on it. I thought that might be a safe way for us to get us down a couple of hundred vertical feet, and then we'd see. So we went down through the trees and further down on this open slope. I was making telemark turns, which was fun. Lynnie was going down in zig-zags, back and forth, back and forth.

LM: Of course I kept falling down because I was tired, cold, wet, and I still had that damn pack which weighed more because it was soaked. Then we heard the helicopter.

HW: Steve Hickman was the district ranger at Badger Pass then. He knew we had been missing for a few days. There was a break in the storm, so he sent a helicopter with our friends George Durkee and Dave Norris.

LM: They saw tele tracks and zig-zags and they knew it had to be Lynn and Howard.

HW: But they couldn't see us, and at that point, it didn't make any difference, because we were a couple of hours from getting out. The last part was hard, though, because when holes opened up in the clouds, sun torched the surface of the snow. With wet snow on top and dry snow underneath, we started to drag snow like you couldn't believe on the total length of both skis, pounds and pounds of it as we headed up towards Mammoth Pass. Finally we got to the little lodge with a fireplace at Tamarack Lake around dark.

LM: When he went to the bathroom, I took my skis off and was about to put them right in the fireplace! I was that close when he came out and said, "No, don't burn them!" After that, I told anybody worried about their weight to go on a trip with Howard.

HW: It was a hard go, no question. After two and a half days of real cruising, we had three and a half days of real schlogging. Today people bring electronics to protect themselves from these kinds of events. I suppose I'd bring a compass if I had it to do over again. Maybe we could have hunkered down for a day and restored ourselves, but my tendency is to keep moving and keep yourself warm even when you get sandbagged by a weather forecast.

LM: I think the hypothermia would have been worse if we had stopped. Don't depend on the weather forecast. That was a lesson, and bring more food. Bring extra for that margin of safety.
   Just before we married, the greatest lesson of this trip for me was finding out that even under pressure we were always kind to one another. In the hardest moments, we were both very considerate. I didn't say, "Damn it, Howard, how did you get me into this?" He didn't say, "Lynn, you're going too slow!" We helped each other out as best we could and didn't start the blame game. That was a real blessing.

HW: A trip like this could have broken other people apart, but Lynn was durable, steady and consistent. She was very accepting of the situation, of me and my judgment, good and bad. There were certainly times when someone could have gotten angry, but that never happened. I really couldn't ask for more.

LM: I never did another trans-Sierra. I think I'd rather sit in the bathroom and hit myself with a lead pipe! Though I went into the hut for years after that. I got some Fischer skis that weren't made of wood. The snow clumps a lot less under them. We started using skins, which are a godsend. The technology changed and made things quite a bit easier. I'm not very graceful, but I do love getting on a pair of skis and coming down hills.

HW: Travel like this, there's a lot of perseverance in it. Some people just get mentally exhausted, plodding and dragging snow day after day, but I just love to be out. I love to break trail. It keeps you in good shape. The people are wonderful and the quiet is wonderful. There's nothing about it I don't like. The Sierra is pretty forgiving. It's the gentle wilderness, and there's a lot of slack out there. I always said I never had a bad trip, and I still look at this one as not a bad trip.

Dale Bard:
"In the Dead of Winter"

A fixture of Yosemite in the 1970s, Dale Bard became famous for both his bold climbing and his frugal lifestyle. Bard lived in a converted bakery van and sustained himself on peanut butter and potatoes for weeks at a time, earning kudos from Climbing Magazine for perfecting the "dirtbag" lifestyle. Though with first ascents of Half Dome's Bushido and El Capitan's Sea of Dreams and Sunkist routes to his credit, the climber wrote his name indelibly in the record book.

Bard describes in glowing terms a formidable ski trek that most would consider a grueling ordeal. With companion Nadim Melkonian, the 23-year-old outdoorsman set out to trace the John Muir Trail in January of 1976. Expecting good weather and fast conditions, the pair planned to finish in three weeks. But storms repeatedly pounded the skiers who survived multiple avalanches and dire food shortages on a journey more than twice as long as expected.

When I was young and foolish, Nadim Melkonian and I took a fairly extensive ski trip through the mountains, about 250 miles. We had planned to go in the dead of winter, because I was a knucklehead and wanted a true winter ski tour. We did the High Route from Sequoia National Park to Yosemite Valley. We came in on the west from an area called Panther Gap, over the Sierras to Mt. Whitney, and then we grabbed the John Muir Trail, sort of, because of course you can't see it in winter.

I wasn't supposed to ski with Nadim, but his partner bailed out on him. Nadim was bummed and moping around. He had already cached all this food along the route. So on a lark I decided to go with him. I had no gear, so I went down to the mountain shop and bought everything I needed. At that time, I had an alpine skiing background, not any cross country skiing experience per se. The only downside was the equipment was so different. But once you know how to ski, you just go skiing. I got on a pair of Atomics, truly skinny, metal-edged skis I had to repair multiple times on the trip. We left on Jan. 20 and planned to take 21 days. We were gone 44.

At the time, Nadim was the Snow Creek cabin ranger, which was most helpful. We got to use a lot of the wilderness rangers' cabins along the way to stash our food. Every once in a while, we actually got to spend a night in a cabin, which was cool. We had one the first night, and one by Charlotte Dome, and another by University Peak. So for a while it was almost like hut skiing, and we got spoiled.

We made it over Forester Pass before we got nailed by the first storm. We were on schedule, moving fast. We thought it would be no problem to make 15 or 20 miles per day. Then once we got over Forester, four feet of snow dumped on us. We kept skiing, but all hell broke loose at Muir Pass. A huge storm nailed us and pinned us down for three days. We pitched our tent inside the John Muir Hut, a stone structure there which kept us out of the whiteout. But we were running out of food and had to get to our next cache.

More than 12 feet of snow came down in two days. We were breaking trail chest-deep. This is pre-GPS and we got totally disoriented in Goddard Canyon. It got dark and we were still in whiteout conditions. We set up our dome tent in a grove of trees. You could just hear the avalanches kicking down all around us. We heard this one come down pretty loud and the walls of our tent started getting spattered. An avalanche produces quite a gust of wind. Later, Nadim looks at his watch. Even though it's pitch black, he says, "Dale, it's 8 in the morning." I say, "That's ridiculous!" We unzipped the door of the tent and there's a wall of snow there. What happened was the avalanche broke up as it hit the trees but still buried our tent under five feet of snow. We had to shovel the snow into the tent to dig out, and then we had to dig the snow back out of the tent again. We had just one small snow shovel so that took a couple of hours. It was really hilarious and we kept laughing at each other. We were totally

Mt. Ritter (left) and Banner Peak (right) near Mammoth Lakes

lucky and dodged a bullet. We were just far enough out of the avalanche's path. As I look back on it, we should have died. Obviously we were idiots as far as avalanche awareness goes. The next day a second avalanche buried us up to our knees.

At this point, we were getting very close to not making it. We survived on one tea bag and half a stick of butter for three days. We were way off course and finally we had to break into this dude ranch. We were so hungry and when we broke in there was a jar of peanut butter on the table. Neither one of us could open it because our cold hands didn't work. So we sat in the hot springs there and salivated over the jar until we had the strength and the coordination to open it. Inside the ranch there was a 55-gallon drum full of food sealed up for the fall. We opened it up and resupplied and that enabled us to get to our next food cache. If we hadn't made it to the dude ranch, I think it would have been pretty critical. I left a note with my address saying what we had done and to contact me for damages. I left $10 I had with me. They saved our asses so I figured it was the least I could do.

Ten more feet of snow dumped while we were there. Finally the weather cleared and we left the ranch. Then this helicopter came cruising by us. There were a lot of rescues going on in the mountains at that time because the storm caught a lot of folks unprepared. The pilot held a hover and asked, did we want a rescue? We said, "Hell no, we're fine!" By that point we were absolutely determined.

And so we went on to our next food cache, which was 20 feet down in the snow. We dug down and got that and kept on skiing. In a way, I hated it when we got to a food cache. It bummed me out because I'd have a beautiful light pack, and then when we got the food, I'd have to carry 45 pounds again. But every cache had a little treat, like Oreos or M&Ms, so we knew we'd get something special and that made us happy.

On a tour that long, you get used to it, kind of like big wall climbing. You get up in the morning and ski until dark. At the end of the day, you make camp and do your chores and go to bed. Then you get up and go again. It's like a 9 to 5 job.

We were caught in more storms and whiteouts after that. It was a pretty epic year. We ran out of food again. We managed to come in behind Mammoth Lakes. There was another hot springs area that had a cabin, and we broke into that and got more food. There was a pay phone there and though we had no money, I called collect and luckily reached my girlfriend Janet. By this time we were 20 days late and everybody thought we were dead. So she was glad to hear from me although she was mad at first.

We got nailed by a horrendous storm on the back side of Mammoth and contemplated skiing out. I looked at Nadim and said, "We've been fighting for this trip the whole time, and there's maybe 45 miles to go." He looked at me and we agreed to keep on going. We wanted it and by that time we had skied almost 200 miles. What's another 45? It seemed like a mere pittance. We were just three days from Tuolumne even with the trail breaking we had to do.

The weather broke and we had some blue bird days. Finally we hit Tuolumne Meadows. We were out of food again but knew of the wilderness post up there. We really surprised the rangers there when we pulled up. "Where are you coming from?" they asked. When we told them, they looked at us like we were nuts. Anne Macquarie and

Lyell Canyon   Photo: Cliff DeYoung

her husband Chas took such good care of us. They made us this wonderful meal with fresh bread. We stayed two days there. We were in heaven and didn't want to leave.

Then we just skied back into the Valley. It was very surreal when we got a little bit below Snow Creek cabin. When we put our skis on our packs and hiked on dirt, that was a very interesting thing after so long in the snow. And it was just weird to see people again. I went to see Janet at the restaurant in the Valley where she worked as a waitress. By this time I was sub-100 pounds. Everyone looked at us like we were ghosts or something. Janet dropped everything and ran over and put a wet one on me in front of the entire restaurant. Then she sat me down and fed me. I had a craving for hot chocolate and whipped cream. I must have had ten cups of that stuff in a row!

Next spring, I'm in Yosemite and I got a letter in the mail from the dude ranch people. The note said they were glad to help out and they returned my $10!

I never looked at it as life-threatening. It was something where we persevered. Nadim was a good partner to hang with, real solid. I learned a lot about skiing and became a better skier. I was such a knucklehead back then. I thought I was invincible, so I did stupid tricks all the way through the trip in steep, scary bowls. I look at those bowls today and there's no way I would do that again.

As I've told many people, I don't plan an epic. I didn't plan this to be an epic. Sometimes you've just got to work through it. It was just a good adventure and fun to be out there.

Marty McDonnell:
"Dance with the Dragon"

"Mind your own business" is an adage that carries weight outdoors. Rafters and other enthusiasts are a friendly though independent lot and rarely crave unsolicited advice. After all, solitude and privacy contribute to the outdoors' appeal. But what circumstances call for one to break that silence?

That question faced Marty McDonnell, then 28, on the Stanislaus River in the stormy spring of 1978. A whitewater pioneer, a seasoned guide and founder of Sierra Mac River Trips, McDonnell and a crack crew braved the Camp 9 Parrott's Ferry run as it raged many times greater than the river's normal volume. However, a less-prepared party created the rafters' greatest challenge that day.

I f you saw a conspicuous crack in the window of a jet plane you were about to board, what would you do? Getting sucked out the plane's window at 32,000 feet, you could reasonably predict your end was near. Would you warn others of the apparent danger? Would you refuse to get on the plane? But what if you were wrong and overreacted? Who are you to question the expertise of the airline's quality control? Questions like these swirl inside my mind as I remember the story of a pivotal day on the Stanislaus River.

A perfect storm had arrived, and we were ready for it. It had been snowing non-stop for over a week in the high country northwest of Yosemite and now a tropical deluge was melting it away like butter in a hot frying pan. Boaters like us lived for such times, when the river reached its maximum level and we could test our skills and equipment to the limit while having the ride of our lives.

I had assembled an ideal crew to match the demands of a trip riding the dragon's back of a river in flood. We were six well-honed boaters in two state-of-the-art rafts, self-bailing oar rigs called Huck Finns designed and built by the legendary Bryce Whitmore in 1966. Huck Finns look like a giant air mattress with four tubes laced together, with one person rowing a pair of ten-foot oars from the stern, and two nimble souls near the bow jumping on the ever-changing high side of the boat to keep it from flipping. I captained one boat, and my longtime navigational partner Chris Condon led the other.

We were joined by fellow Sierra foothill residents Mike Nelson and Tom Cornett, both intrepid entrepreneurs and partners in crime on several eccentric whitewater expeditions. Like me, they had migrated from the northern California coast and had lots of experience surfing the big waves of the Pacific. Mark Dubois and Fred Dennis, early pioneers of the river conservation movement and highly skilled navigators in their own right, had come to gawk at the mesmerizing floodwaters and were easily enticed to join us. This same veteran group in 1973 had made the first descent of the Cherry Creek / Upper Tuolumne run (now considered the most challenging commercial rafting run in the US) in self-bailing catarafts I designed and built for the task. I had been running high water trips on the Stan and the nearby Tuolumne for more than 13 years and was at the top of my game.

In spite of the pounding rain, we had an excellent run the first day. The river was flowing around 14,000 cubic feet per second (cfs), 12 times the normal summertime level. The shoreline, a lethal tangle of fallen trees, overhanging branches and swift current, was to be avoided at all costs. But if you stayed out in middle on the writhing spine of the rampaging dragon, you could dance with her, and that we did. On the next day we came back for more.

As we were blowing up our rafts at the Camp 9 put-in, the intensity of the storm increased. The rain was so thick that those of us with glasses couldn't see. The narrow seams in the cliffs above us, normally dry, gushed with torrential runoff and created dramatic waterfalls. The river had risen so fast that the parking lot was under nearly a foot of water. The back eddy at the put-in was on full boil. The raging upstream current crashed headfirst into the full force of the down-stream current as it careened around a bridge abutment, creating a ferocious four-foot high wall of water that needed to be traversed in order to get into the main current. The Stan roared past us at 18,000 cfs. By the time we pushed off it neared 23,000, and the river peaked that day around 28,000. That is enough water to fill a container the size of a football field with ten feet of water in about 21 seconds.

But we were not the only boaters launching a trip that day. Another group of river guides prepared for an overnight excursion just behind us. Since we were at the higher end of the "acceptable level of risk" for whitewater boating on the Stan, I had a short chat with them while we were all rigging. They were professional guides, so I didn't say much but I did tell them about our run the day before and departed with a "have fun."

As we were getting into our final take-off position, I noticed that their loads were inordinately large and unwieldy, too big for the task at hand. They even had a pile of folded lawn chairs (also known as death traps) strapped to the top, a sure sign that they had little idea of what they were doing. You could barely see the rowers' heads through their haystacks of gear. Even more troubling, none of them wore wetsuits, an absolute necessity on high water trips where getting catapaulted into a frigid river is a very real possibility.

Breaking that eddy fence (or I should say a randomly oscillating four-foot water wall) was one of the biggest challenges of the day. From then on, the main driving force of the river looked pretty clean. As we flushed out into the main current making a sharp U-turn downstream, I worried about the other boaters' fate. I looked over my shoulder to see them with their thumbs up, cheering us on through the grey curtain. I couldn't help but think that they would be in trouble very soon. But my focus turned to the task at hand: staying on line.

Death Rock got its name in the late 1960s after a springtime outing went very wrong. A group of scouts had each made their own "rafts," glorified inner tubes with glued-in floors in which the boys sat cross legged, enveloped in rain ponchos, secured around their waists with rope and tied again to the bottom of the tubes.

The young boys took off from shore in the promising sunshine with no idea what they were up against. The water was cold and high. Few, if any, wore lifejackets. Like a wayward school of guppies, the boys were quickly whisked away by the swift current and scattered in all directions, totally out of control. Fishermen dotting the shoreline hauled them out the best they could, but one was not so lucky. He drifted right into the hole at the then-unnamed Death Rock, immediately flipped over, and was caught in the backwash of the slurping maw. Bryce Whitmore, the first outfitter on the Stan, grabbed him just above Devil's Staircase, but by that time he was dead. The force of the hydraulics had turned the poncho into a ballooning sea anchor, pinching him off around the base of his spine so that his torso had almost completely collapsed to the size of his backbone. The foolhardy adventure is well-known among river guides of the Stan.

As we approached Death Rock, we saw that it was now fully submerged. This created a huge sucking hole that could easily swallow several Winnebagos at once. The trees along the shoreline had major rapids flowing through them with a deadly thrashing of straining limbs and debris. Since we knew what to expect, we made the move early on to avoid the worst of it.

The first place we could safely stop was three miles downstream, just below the confluence with Rose Creek and opposite the Cataract Cement Plant overlook, 1,200 vertical feet above. With intuition born of many years on the river, Chris and I smelled trouble and decided to wait. I hovered on the eddy line, working it back and forth, up and down, in circles and angles, waiting. Chris pulled over to an open area of the rollicking shoreline, doing all he could to stay in one place. Within minutes, a few oars, an ice chest and other rafting flotsam came floating by, including a lifeless lump of humanity with only the pate of his head barely visible from the top of his lifejacket.

I peeled out into the current making chase to intercept the body as it drifted toward the ugly strainers above Mother Rapid. If he wasn't already dead, they would certainly do him in, locking him in their lethal web and keeping his head underwater for good. In desperate voices we yelled at the body to "swim right, swim right!" Miraculously, his arms actually started flopping in the correct direction, and he narrowly missed an ugly fate.

He was in the main current now and immediately picked up speed as he entered the freight train of standing waves below. It would be extremely difficult for even the most seasoned of guides to survive a swim like this especially after all he had been through already. I was doing all I could to catch him, rowing backwards through the thunderous wave train at full speed, deflecting the current to my advantage and trying to stay on line so that we wouldn't become victims of high water ourselves. Hot pursuit of a body in a whitewater river requires perfect timing and exceptional navigation. Bodies are like submarines, plowing through rapids at a surprisingly fast clip. Rafts are slower, subject to the various currents, waves and other river features that hinder speedy downstream progress. Walls of water kept pushing us back upstream and slowed our pursuit. He was still out in front, headed full steam toward Razor Back. Finally we caught up to him just above the entry turn and hauled his nearly-lifeless body aboard as I swung into shore. The guy wasn't wearing a wetsuit and suffered from severe hypothermia. He vomited and passed out. We got him into a sleeping bag and took turns sharing our body warmth with him.

After a while he came round and told us of his epic. Within the first five minutes he had flipped in the hole at Death Rock, and like a good river guide, crawled onto the top of his overturned raft to assist the rescue. Unfortunately the rescue didn't come and he was carried by the merciless river into the powerful laterals at the Rose Creek confluence, where he flipped a second time.

We stabilized his condition and tended to his trauma the best we could. A few very wet and cold hours later, his group finally caught up to us, shaken up from their own dramas but all intact and very happy to see him standing on the shore with us. Then their trip fell apart. Most of the passengers hiked out and those who remained paralleled our boats to the takeout at Parrott's Ferry, which we almost missed due to thick fog that settled into the canyon.

I don't remember his name, but every once in a while we meet at a Friends of the River conference or on the banks of the Tuolumne. Each time he makes a point of giving me a hug and a big smile of thanks, reminding me that I saved his life. It's an interesting energy exchange that makes me slightly uncomfortable, as I only did what comes naturally to most people who spend their lives with rivers. I do know that I used every bit of my expertise during that rescue which marked a peak in the arc of my performance and the culmination of years of experience running high water trips. We had the right crew, the right equipment and the right blend of strength, skill, foresight, and chutzpah required to make a successful interception and dance with the dragon.

Forty-five years of river running has taught me that in any given rapid, even the shortest distance must be navigated with wisdom and respect, and there is no substitute for the long and bumpy road of experience … and I wouldn't get on that plane!

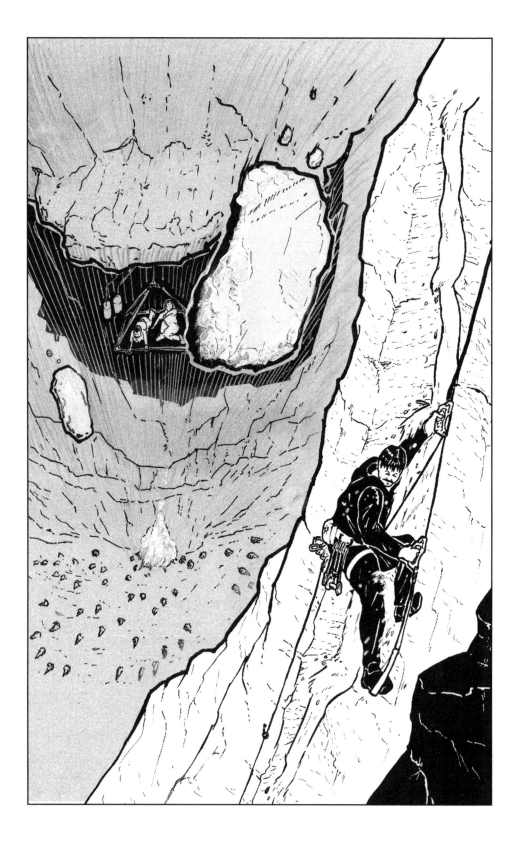

Errett Allen:
"Nature's Power"

Backpacker Errett Allen hiked north on the Pacific Crest Trail from Southern California in the spring of 1974. Six weeks and 550 miles later, he detoured into Yosemite Valley to rest an injured knee. The visit transformed the "weekend warrior" who moved into Camp 4 for most of the next six years to test himself against Sierra granite. In later years Allen prolifically established first ascents, many on difficult and rarely-repeated Tuolumne Meadows routes like Voyager, Breaking Wind and Blue Moon.

None of the climber's adventures tested him more severely than El Capitan's New Dawn line (5.9/A4)[1]. A worthy 29-pitch challenge in good conditions, the route becomes a nearly-unclimbable waterfall in rain and a death-trap in snow. Falling rock and ice added still more peril to the life-and-death struggle which Allen, 27, and partner Mike Corbett faced in November of 1978.

I had no particular desire to suffer in wintertime, but fall was coming to a close and Mike Corbett and I wanted to squeeze in a wall climb. We really wanted to climb El Cap, which is such an immense challenge and takes so much preparation. New Dawn itself is a beautiful line, with a blank dihedral section that's quite impressive, and Mike and I both had admiration for Warren Harding, who'd climbed it before.

The fact that we attempted it in November season required extra planning and preparation. Short days, long cold nights and the possibility of a winter storm all had to be accounted for in our scheme.

1. For an explanation of climbing ratings, see page 189.

In addition, an aspect of the climb added to our potential problems. The route makes a long traverse to the right involving roped pendulums from bolts. This places climbers directly above a huge, steeply-overhanging section of rock. Without the placement of many additional bolts that we didn't have, the pendulums would be difficult if not impossible to reverse. Any retreat would be difficult even for experienced and healthy climbers. With either of us injured, it would be impossible. And if a winter storm caught us above this point, we would be forced to sit it out.

Our gear included rain suits, one down sleeping bag, a synthetic half bag, down jackets, bivvy sacs and enough layers of wool to swath 30 sheep. We also acquired (ahem) a primitive steel and canvas portable ledge; metal cots bolted to the walls in Housekeeping Camp served that purpose before climbers could buy a commercial portaledge. A two-man tube tent was rigged with duct tape as a rain fly. With the usual ton of iron, food and water for six days, our gear easily exceeded 200 pounds. For good measure I threw in my camera and a copy of "Atlas Shrugged" to read during those long winter nights.

We fixed ropes on the first three pitches and took forever doing all the borrowing, buying, organizing and packing that was necessary. This also helped delay the day of reckoning. We decided to fix one more pitch to boost our morale. Finally out of excuses, we blasted off Nov. 28 on a clear day with nothing but sun in the forecast.

Neither of us were early risers and it was nearly dark by the time we ascended our fixed lines and climbed the next three pitches. This was just as well since we were on Lay Lady Ledge – a large, comfortable place to camp. The climbing was easy so far and the weather was cold but clear. We knew at this time of year there are only a few hours of warm weather on this side of El Cap. Even when sunny, the mornings were cold, and just as things warmed up, the sun set behind The Nose and we would get cold again. The entire time we were on the route, temperatures on the Valley floor dipped into the low 20s at night.

The next day dawned clear and sunny and we were soon in the groove, smoothly sailing upward. I had one minor mishap on the day's third pitch. The belay at the top is the ledge atop El Cap Towers

– a narrow but long, flat and comfortable ledge. The anchors there at the time were three old bolts, probably placed by Harding 20 years earlier, none of which inspired confidence. I selected one which looked strongest to haul our bags on. As I strained to move them over a difficult section, the bolt suddenly pulled out. I flew back and found myself dangling in space, pulled down by the weight of the bags but held up by my tether to another bolt. After finishing the haul from this difficult position, we set up camp on the ledge. We fixed the next two and a half pitches before dark and then settled down for a comfortable night on El Cap Towers.

Another clear cold morning found us involved on the pendulum traverse and we were soon swinging like yoyos on a steep and exposed wall. After the traverse we were in a series of barely discernable and very shallow thin cracks that shoot up for several hundred feet. The climbing here is easy aid, but tenuous, involving many moves on Harding's rivets[2] that only penetrate the rock one quarter inch. We knew from word of mouth around Camp 4 that we had to thread small wired stoppers over the heads of these rivets to clip our aid ladders in, but discovered to our chagrin that only the tiniest wired stoppers would work. We only had two of those. So we had to leapfrog our carabiners without leaving anything clipped in for protection behind us. Fully stimulated, we arrived at our next bivvy site called Wino Towers.

A few empty wine bottles we found here attested to the low moral character of our predecessors and we promptly broke out our own bottle. The ledge here is small, uneven and uncomfortable so our portaledge came into play for the first time. Though the sky was clear we set up the rain fly to shelter us. All day long as we climbed we were showered by steadily increasing marble-sized drops from a waterfall on the rim. Unnoticed in the morning, the sun would slowly increase melting on top until by mid-afternoon there would be a steady stream. The shower hit us sporadically up to this point and depended on how the wind was blowing. We relaxed that night listening to the pitter-patter of drops hitting our rain fly, oblivious to the danger awaiting us.

---

2. rivet: a bolt lacking the usual hanger for placing carabiners, offering climbers only limited use for protection

Again the sun greeted us in the morning. We packed our gear slowly with stiff limbs and sore hands and began climbing. Wind had picked up overnight and drops hit us early. After I led the day's first pitch, Mike began the second under an increasing barrage of water. As I started cleaning the pitch, the wind grew stronger and the shower got serious. Reaching the belay, I found Mike shivering uncontrollably and fumbling in the bags for our rain gear. I was still warm from cleaning the pitch but quickly I began to shiver, too. The drenching became worse by the minute and the sun took this opportunity to set behind The Nose.

We were in dire straits and would soon be hypothermic. About 30 feet above us was a bulge of rock that afforded protection from the shower so we climbed up there, hauled our gear up and quickly set up our portaledge and rain fly. To our dismay we discovered that all of our bivvy gear was soaking wet! We had been careless about packing it that morning. Plus, the practice at that time was to put bivvy gear in garbage bags to keep it dry, but in the course of packing and unpacking, holes had torn in the plastic. Everything had become soaked. Fortunately we had lots of wool garments and after wringing them out as much as we could, we donned all of them. Facing each other on the narrow portaledge, we rubbed our hands and each other's completely numb feet. Slowly and painfully, warmth returned to our extremities and we assessed our situation.

My sleeping bag, Mike's half bag and our down jackets were no longer soaking wet. They were now frozen lumps of ice, completely useless. The wool we wore was slowly drying out, however, and we were warming up in our shelter. Retreat was completely impractical but we felt that our situation was not desperate and decided to sit out the afternoon and night. Hopefully with good weather we could continue to the top. That night was the longest and coldest bivouac of my life. With nothing but our wool to keep us from freezing, we spent the whole night rubbing what little warmth we could into our hands, feet and limbs. Sleep was impossible.

The sun rising bright and clear the next morning was a most beautiful sight. The waterfall abated overnight as the temperature dropped, freezing everything but us. We wasted no time packing and hurried to climb while we could do it dry and warm. Fortunate-

New Dawn on El Capitan

ly the next two pitches angled away from the waterfall. The climbing was slow, though, as four days of climbing and a cold, sleepless bivvy took a toll on our stamina. At every belay, we broke out some frozen pieces of bivvy gear and hung them from a rope clothesline, making El Cap look like an inner city slum. We must have been a sight from El Cap Meadow especially since we were the only guys stupid enough to be up there. Our down items never thawed in the cold weather, and we never got to use them the rest of the climb. That day we only completed three and a half pitches before nightfall – our slowest day so far. The one thing that lifted our spirits somewhat was that Mike's half bag did thaw out enough to use for our next bivvy. So that night saw us ensconced on our portaledge with all four legs in one small half bag, not warm but better off than the night before. We were now 23 pitches off the deck and only five from the top.

High winds and whipping snow woke us the next morning before dawn. Snow was already piling up on our rain fly and gear and we wondered why we had ever taken up this stupid sport. We were about 100 feet below a small roof which was further protected by a huge roof 30 feet higher. Without even packing our bags, we climbed up under the first roof, hauled our junk and set up a new camp much more protected from the storm. Snow fell heavily and continuously throughout the day. Under the roof we were well protected with only an occasional gust of wind strong enough to blow snow over us. If it wasn't for our exposed position and dwindling food, it would have been a pleasure to take a rest day. We had brought enough food for six days and this was our sixth day. We worried the storm might last several days so we tried to eat as little as possible. With strict rationing, we could stretch our supply for another couple days. The problem was the cold – it was more difficult to stay warm with no calories to burn. But for the moment we were protected, warm and safe.

I had read over half of my book by this time and tore it in half to give Mike something to relieve the boredom. Some of our friends came down to the meadow that day to ask if we were all right and yell encouragement. We shouted back that we were okay and didn't want a rescue. Satisfied, they went back to the restaurants, bars and other amenities in the Valley. We spent the day as couch potatoes, reading, sleeping and daydreaming of warm beds and sumptuous feasts. An occasional foray outside the rain fly for nature's call had to suffice to stretch stiff and sore muscles.

Though it snowed all day and most of the night, towards dawn it began to clear. To our delight, the sun rose and began to work its magic on our cold bodies. Our lighthearted attitude soon turned to dread as the sun also worked its magic on the thick snow and ice plastered to El Cap's rim. A few hail-sized chunks fell past us. Soon larger chunks followed. We thought we would be safe under our small roof until a new phenomenon began. Blocks of ice two to four feet thick and as long and wide as railroad boxcars began to peel off the rim. They would flip over and over like playing cards, making an incredibly loud and dreadful whoosh with each flip. They fell in huge spirals that tracked far out from the wall and then tracked back in. More often than not, they smashed into the wall with great force breaking into thousands of pieces which showered the forest below.

We quickly packed up and climbed the remaining 30 feet to the huge roof above us where we had much better protection from the falling ice. There we watched the most amazing show of nature's power I have ever seen. To poke our heads out above the roof would have been suicide. Some ice slabs tracked halfway out to the meadow and crashed into the forest hundreds of feet from the wall. Some blocks tracked directly past us, unseen and unheard until suddenly they shot by with a terrifying whoosh that sent shivers up my spine. Around noon the ice fall abated. Since half the day was already gone, we resigned to spending another night on the wall.

The pitch above the roof provided more entertainment. It was aid climbing in a thin crack in a shallow dihedral. Near the top of the pitch, a spring gushed water which fell down the dihedral. Quickly freezing, the water filled the crack and covered the wall with a thick coating of hard ice. Mike took this lead and I could tell from many falling chunks of ice and his loud cursing that things weren't pleasant. In order to get gear placements in that crack, Mike had to continually chip out the ice with a hammer and piton.

A long time later I heard his distant "off belay" and now it was time for my fun. I put my ascenders on the rope and when I turned the corner of the roof, I was presented with a nasty sight. The rope and all of our gear was frozen to the dihedral under a layer of ice up most of the pitch. Old-style Jumars were famous back then for not working well on frozen ropes. The teeth on the Jumars' cams that normally grip the rope will quickly jam up with ice. Normally in any scary situation when following an aid pitch with Jumars, climbers will "tie in short." This means you tie directly into the rope every so often so that if your Jumars fail, you will not fall all the way to the end of the rope. In this situation the rope was frozen so hard that it was a major effort, but I took the time to tie those knots.

For every placement of the Jumars I had to first scrape off as much ice as I could with my fingernails, place the Jumar and gingerly test it before committing full weight to it. I frequently had to remove a Jumar from the rope to chip ice. Chipping the rope and the gear out of the frozen dihedral and crack wasn't much fun either. All the time I cleaned this pitch, the spring soaked me just as it had soaked Mike. At least we were still in the sun. We could wring the water out of our clothes and continue climbing. We reached a small bivvy ledge and set up camp for another night, three pitches from the top.

The sun rose on our eighth day on the wall and it was very hard to coax our tired, sore, cold and hungry bodies off the ledge. We only had a few crumbs of bread for breakfast but the thought of the top so close spurred us on. The second pitch required aid with pitons behind a thin flake. Leading the pitch, Mike was about 25 feet directly above me hammering a piton when I heard a crunching sound. I looked up just in time for a 20-pound rock to slam me in the face. A chunk of the flake Mike had been nailing broke off. The right side of my face from forehead to chin became a bleeding and bruised mess as I learned what it's like to be hit by a baseball bat.

I put a good scare into Mike. He told me later that he thought I had been knocked out or even killed. I determined I didn't have any broken bones and reassured Mike I was okay. He continued the pitch. It was a really good thing I had looked up when I did or I would have been hit squarely on the top of my head, perhaps receiving a concussion or skull fracture. As it was I wore an attractive mask of scabs and scars for a while. One more sore spot on my body just blended in with the rest.

Mike graciously offered to lead the last pitch. With blood still running into my eyes, I concurred. Before long we pulled on top of the Captain at 11 a.m. on our eighth day. Though tired, sore, hungry and weak, we were completely elated at having survived and accomplished our goal through so much adversity. Having forgotten how to walk in the last eight days, we stumbled around and fumbled to pack our bags. We bantered about eating in a restaurant, sipping a drink in the bar and sleeping in a dry, warm bed in the evening to come. We thought our hardships were over and in just a few hours we would be surrounded by our friends and the comforts of the Valley. Such are the delusions of starved and confused minds.

We did have enough brain cells left to recognize we would have to be careful getting back to the Valley. Any experienced climber knows the climb ends only when you are safely back down where it started. The storm turned the East Ledges descent into an icy deathtrap. The alternative was to hike four miles to the Yosemite Falls Trail and then another four miles down to the Valley. While sorting our gear, we decided to leave most behind to carry as little as possible. Our heavy portaledge that had done so much to keep us alive, we tossed off the edge and watched as it flipped over and over, arcing in a spiral as it fell and reminding us of the ice from a few days before.

At first the hiking was on easy level ground, but two feet of fresh snow made it difficult in our exhausted state. After a mile or so, we faced an uphill section that rises to the shoulder of Eagle Peak. We soon found ourselves in a field of manzanita hidden under the snow. Mike sank to his knees most steps, and I would often plunge further even when using his tracks. Our feet become tangled in the manzanita, making progress excruciatingly slow. We got soaked from head to foot once again. Utterly exhausted, I stopped to rest and Mike was soon far ahead and out of sight. Eventually I crested the hill and followed Mike's tracks. As the sun was about to set and the temperature dropped, I found Mike curled up under a rock and shivering uncontrollably. He was exhausted and couldn't continue. I was in the same boat.

I set down my pack and pulled out my survival sack containing a water-proof container of matches. There were a couple of dead trees nearby with large dry branches but we had no kindling and the forest floor was covered with snow. We wasted several matches trying to light small pieces of wood without success until I remembered that I had my book in the pack. We tore "Atlas Shrugged" to pieces and soon had a small fire going. Barbecuing our clothing on a spit over the fire, we managed to dry it out. Living to a ripe old age felt a real possibility again. I intended to stay awake all night tending the fire but exhaustion got the best of us and we awoke shivering at dawn.

Within ten minutes of starting out we encountered Yosemite Creek and turned downstream to follow the trail to the Valley. We were only about a hundred yards above the falls and soon stumbled down the switchbacks on frozen feet. Halfway down, we ran into Mike's girlfriend Lisa who was very concerned that we hadn't shown up the day before. There had been talk of mobilizing a search for us. Before long we were back in Camp 4, surrounded by friends eager to hear our tale.

For several years, I suffered from poor circulation in my toes but my face healed nicely and fortunately I turned out no uglier than before. Did I mention that this was my first El Cap route?

I learned some valuable lessons on this climb. We could have been better prepared with waterproof gear and a stove, and we could have packed better so our stuff didn't become soaked and frozen. I didn't learn the most important lesson, as I went on to climb El Cap several more times. But I never did another winter ascent. From then on, I climbed The Captain only in warm, sunny weather.

John Bachar:
"I Got Away with One"

Risk comes with the territory for mountaineers, but none embraced peril like free soloist John Bachar. The climber pioneered the bold style of scaling rocks as hard as 5.13 not only without a partner, but also without rope or protective gear. Again and again, Bachar shocked the outdoors community with his ropeless ascents of such routes as New Dimensions (5.11a), The Nabisco Wall (5.11c), and the East Buttress of Lower Cathedral Rock, a "gnarly" 12-pitch affair more than 1,400 feet tall. Rigorously trained and supremely confident, Bachar once posted a note in Yosemite with this brash offer: "$10,000 reward for anyone who can follow me for one full day." Though many world-class climbers in residence were perpetually broke, none dared take the challenge.

Yet even Bachar had his white-knuckle moments. Here he describes one from The Moratorium, a four-pitch, 5.11b climb near El Capitan which he free soloed in 1980 at age 23. As if climbing alone and unprotected wasn't challenging enough, Bachar scaled the route on sight, meaning he had never climbed it before or even witnessed another attempt it. The result made even the master of free soloing question the wisdom of the practice.

B ack in the early 70s, nobody really soloed above 5.7 or 5.8. That was just considered insane, stupid, foolish, whatever. But one day in Joshua Tree, John Long came up to me and said, "Hey, let's go do Double Cross" (5.7+).

"Yeah, cool man, let's go do it," I said. We started walking in different directions.

"Where you going?" he says.

"I'm going to get the rope," I say.

"Oh no, we're not using ropes," he says.

"Maybe you're not, but I am!"

Then he goes, "Hey, look at it this way, Bachar. If you top rope that thing 100 times, how many times would you fall?"

I say, "Never."

And he says, "All right then, let's go." For some reason, that made sense to me, so we did it.

I'm up there without a rope, and I'm thinking, "This is just nuts." I don't belong here without a rope. All of a sudden, I'm just like a lizard or a chipmunk or whatever other animal scrambles around on the rocks. I felt it was totally natural. Lizards and chipmunks do it, they don't fall, and we're probably as smart as lizards or chipmunks. Why shouldn't we be able to do this? And to back it up, if I did this route 100 or 1,000 times I would never fall, ever.

There's a paradigm of thought that you're not supposed to go up there without a rope. The climbing community understands that's not done. On the other hand, almost nobody talks about it to actually reinvestigate the rules and the paradigms and what's acceptable or unacceptable, dangerous or not dangerous. That's something most climbers don't do, but the better climbers do it all the time, because they're always challenging themselves. Every single frontier is broken that way, not only in climbing but also in other activities.

On the one hand, there's this incredible danger. If you fall, you're dead after you're 50 feet off the ground. But on the other hand, you're completely safe. I think, well, if I did this 100 times, I would never fall. If I did this move five feet off the ground, I would never fall. These moves are well within my capability. That's part of it. And there's the feeling that you're doing something that you shouldn't be doing, or you're in a place that most people never go, like being on the moon maybe. I can imagine if you're on the moon, you'd say, "What the hell am I doing here?" But you're there. Free soloing has that sort of intrigue.

The other benefit is that you can do tons of climbing. There's no stopping for belaying. You don't have to stop to place protection. You don't have a giant rack of gear with you. You don't need a partner. You just walk up and climb. I went out soloing all the time in

The Moratorium on Schultz's Ridge

Yosemite. I had a tremendous circuit. I'd do 1,500 feet of climbing and then go back to Camp 4 at about 10 or 11 to find a partner to do something hard with a rope. And the dudes were still there drinking coffee. They hadn't done anything.

I was looking for an on-sight solo. That's the real challenge. That's real free climbing. You know some things about the route, but you've never done it before. And there's no rope. The Moratorium is a 5.11 crack, maybe 500 feet tall. I talked to a few people who had done it. Some go, "It's mellow, man, it's a good time." Other people say, "It's pretty weird at this stemming section up high." Everyone gives a different story, but they're using a rope, so you have to take that into account. I thought it couldn't be that bad. I solo 5.11s all the time in Yosemite. So I started up this corner one day.

I get up a little ways, and there's like this funky stemming problem. I stem out in this dihedral, and there are pretty good holds in a weird pattern. If you do the right sequence, it's not bad. So I think, "That's the stemming they were talking about." I climb through it and I think, "This is cool."

Then I get up a little higher and there's this 5.10d stemming move, and it's way harder. "Oh, it wasn't that first spot. This is what they were talking about!" But if you do it right, use the right technique and the right sequence, it's not bad. I work through that and got to this ledge, and there's a hand crack there, and the climbing gets easier. I think the rest is going to be mellow.

All of a sudden, near the top, I get to this really hard layback section, and I'm just flabbergasted. "Oh my God, those other two things weren't the crux at all, this is the real deal," I think. I stand there for about 10 minutes on this little teeny ledge looking at a right-facing dihedral. You can't get finger locks. It's just a fingertip layback, and all the beta I had was wrong. I was expecting 5.10d, and it's 5.11b. This thing is horrendous, plus I'm wearing EBs, the old climbing shoes before sticky rubber.

I'm looking at the wall and it's a right-facing layback, so your feet are on the right side of the wall. And the right of the wall is this smooth, polished Yosemite granite, no holds at all. On the wall about chest high I do see this little bead, like a pimple, on the rock. I could see that after a couple of moves I might want to put my foot on it, but probably not. It's polished and not the kind of thing I want to put body weight on. I tell myself, "There's no way I'm standing on that thing, no way!"

Finally I decide to go for it. I know this is a move that I shouldn't be doing, it's not secure, but I have to do it, I can't climb down from here. I pull into the layback to see what it's like. I did that probably five times, and it's insecure as hell. Laybacks are one of the hardest things to free solo, because if your feet slip, you're out of there. I pull up and I'm going to reach one more layback hold and then I'm going to get a finger lock, and it should be over in three moves. I'm reaching for the finger lock, and boom! The crack is not big enough to get a finger lock, it's still too thin, and I have to layback another move. "Shit!" After doing that one move, I'm committed. I can't undo it, so I just keep laybacking and look for that bead.

I didn't want to step on that bead because I could slide right off it, but I need a foothold and now I know that I have to use it. I put my foot on it and I have to press on it for all I'm worth. Now I know if I had done this route before, there's no way I would have soloed this thing, ever. But I'm climbing on sight, and you don't know what's going to get tossed at you. I want 100 percent of my concentration on my moves, and now that wasn't happening. There's a little piece of me thinking my foot is going to slip, that I might fall. I'm not in my comfort zone. Normally when I'm free soloing, all I see is a little circle of rock around me. I could be five feet off the ground or 500 feet off the ground, and all I see is my next move, I'm playing with the moves and I'm having fun. At that moment, I was thinking about falling and it wasn't good.

So I put all my weight on the bead, pull up, reach up again, and this time I get a finger lock. Boom! It's solid, and the rest of the climb is hand cracks to the top, no big deal.

At the top, I sat down. I was kind of disoriented. I felt like a hollow shell. I felt like I got away with one. I didn't feel like I conquered it. It let me slip through. I got lucky, like playing blackjack when you have to get 21 and you do. When you scare yourself, it doesn't feel like an accomplishment. It feels like almost being in a car accident. Your heart's beating and you think, "One more inch and I would have been erased from the planet." I couldn't solo for a few days.

People ask me about Moratorium a lot but I'm not proud of that solo. If I had just waltzed through it and that part didn't faze me, I could have told everybody, "Cool climb, no problems," but that didn't happen. The thing about soloing, it's easy to fool other people if you want. No one else is there so you could easily lie about it. But you don't want to fool yourself. You cannot do that. You've got to be really honest with yourself, or you're going to get bit, big time.

After that I thought more carefully about soloing on sight, but I did a lot of other solos. It's immediately very freeing. It's extraordinary. Anybody can get to the summit of El Cap. To me, climbing is as much about style and how you do it.

Obviously hardly anybody free solos, relatively speaking. It never got real popular, and I don't recommend it. For those who choose it, I would say know your limits and don't scare yourself.

Please see the afterword starting on page 183 for an important note about John Bachar.

Royal Robbins:
"The Best Medicine"

Royal Robbins left his mark on Yosemite by leaving as few marks as possible. While achieving historic first ascents including Half Dome's Northwest Face and El Capitan's Salathé Wall, the pioneer promoted an ethic of clean climbing, shunning the overuse of bolts and pitons. Climbers now enjoy scaling Yosemite classics free of excessive alterations thanks largely to the efforts of Robbins and his like-minded contemporaries, though the onset of arthritis led him to redirect his energy toward kayaking in the late 1970s.

Today the Middle Fork of the San Joaquin River carries a rating of Class V+ for extreme danger, dropping nearly 5,000 feet over 32 harrowing miles. Robbins, 45, and companions Doug Tompkins and Reg Lake attempted the first descent over five days in September of 1980. The wild mountain river that plunges over waterfalls and carves through giant boulders in narrow canyons provided the adventure of a lifetime, and the whitewater journey also helped Robbins discover an even greater reward.

C limbing was my number one pursuit, but I got into river running because I developed arthritis. My wrists and ankles started hurting and when I went climbing they would hurt even more. I had been pretty lucky up until then in that I had done a lot and avoided any nasty injuries like broken bones, though it was obvious I couldn't continue climbing like I had been. But I could still boat and paddle, even though it was painful. Kayaking offered an outlet for my energies and my drive to do new things in the outdoors.

The Middle Fork of the San Joaquin River, a trans-Sierra traverse, was a virgin route. Doug Tompkins had a small plane and we flew over the area to look at the river in June of 1981. Clearly it was a serious gorge, very impressive with big walls. In the spring it's just crazy down there, whitewater from beginning to end. You don't want water that big where the drop is so steep. So I went up to take another look with Reg Lake in August from the highest possible put-in. We boated about six miles of the upper part below Shadow Lake down to Devils Postpile National Monument. A week later, we came back with Doug and committed ourselves to the rest of the experience.

As a team we were balanced. Reg was the kayaking expert. Doug, with his intense drive, was the engine. I was the brakeman, to keep the pace leisurely and avoid mistakes. I'd been kayaking somewhat, but I didn't consider myself an expert by any means. It's a good thing we didn't know what we were doing, because a shrewder evaluation of the situation might have led us to say no. Our advantage was that we didn't know enough about it to be as terrified as we should have been.

We put in at Devils Postpile. The San Joaquin begins as a small river, high in the mountains amid pines and firs. We weren't used to that, because in kayaking most of your boating is in the foothills where there's brush. The water started at about 300 cubic feet per second, pretty small but it was big enough to float our boats and give us thrills. The first day got us partway down the gorge past the Postpile and below Rainbow Falls, around which we portaged. When the gradient got too steep, we'd get out of the boats, cross slabs, lower our boats into the river and rappel down, using rock climbing skills. Frankly, we were surprised to get so far without carrying the kayaks more. The grade was steep but forgiving, allowing us to stay on the river in our boats in places where we didn't think we could do that, based on the map. So it was a gift.

On the second day we approached Waterslide Fall, which was a serious section because if you screw it up, you're liable to go over an 80-foot waterfall. We would have carried our boats past it, but there were steep walls on either side. Doug went first and came within five feet of the falls, but you have to come that close to reach an eddy where you can stop. He was hard to scare. I was much easier to frighten. I was terrified of that run. It was really something I would

Rainbow Falls on the Middle Fork of the San Joaquin River

have avoided if I could have, but we didn't have any choice. We had to run it. My heart was pounding, but we each reached the eddy where we could get out and carry our boats around the falls to put in again.

The next big question was the Great Corridor, where the river drops past Balloon Dome into a section called the Granite Crucible. At the beginning of this, we rappelled from a piton past First Falls. Then we had to stop at a drop called Double Chute because we couldn't see all of it from above. We thought it was probably okay, and it probably was, but if it isn't, you're liable to die. That gets your attention. Taking a chance like that is not the way I was raised! We had brought climbing equipment, so if necessary we could have tried to escape the canyon that way, though the walls were thousands of feet high. Finally Reg saved the day by climbing out of his kayak onto a boulder right at the big drop. He looked over the other side and said, "It'll go!" Those were good words to hear. Otherwise one of us probably would have gone anyway, sooner or later. We would have got tired of paddling around in circles in the pool above.

In the beautiful San Joaquin River gorge, we saw things that we never saw anywhere else before or since. We kayaked under a giant chock stone. The river actually ran under a boulder in the canyon. That was the first time I'd ever seen that. We stopped each night next to the river wherever we could see places for sleeping bags and slept under the stars. We packed light, very much like on a climb, and took just nuts, gorp and salami to eat. You feel lucky to have whatever is in your hands, and there's always steak waiting for you at the end.

We descended a series of pool-drop rapids on the last day. You go over a drop, reach a quiet pool where you can recover, then you go for a ways until another drop, and another quiet pool. That was pretty nice, compared to a continuous flow with no pools and no place to recover. We ran into the mouth of Mammoth Pool Reservoir and paddled a few miles on the beautiful blue water to the takeout.

I thought the gorge would be a trade route. I'm surprised it hasn't become more popular. That speaks of its difficulty and challenge. I compare it to the Salathé Wall of El Capitan. That was a great adventure too. This was an adventure like that in that we didn't know what was coming for sure, and there was some risk. If I had to give up all the climbs I've done except for one, it would be Salathé Wall. If I had one river to keep, I would choose the Middle Fork of the San Joaquin, because of the scenery, the adventure, the friendship, the beauty and everything it involved. To us, it was a privilege to be in such a place.

My specialist was pretty pessimistic and didn't say anything about the prospect of my arthritis healing. I was missing my Eskimo roll because of pain in my wrists, and I wondered if it would get worse and force me to stop kayaking, too. But luckily my arthritis went away after a few years and I returned to climbing classic moderates. These days I enjoy both climbing and kayaking. I love the sense of freedom that these sports provide. Every time I climb or paddle, I think I'm lucky to be able to do this. I appreciate these things so much more than I would have if I'd never lost them.

I can't say I have the cure, but I do know that my improvement coincided with my decision not to let arthritis rule my life. I think laughter is the best medicine and we laughed a lot on that trip. I'm a deep believer that the more optimistic you are, the better things go for you. I've been able to achieve things most people consider extraordinary by the power of that principle. If you live with an adventurous, positive attitude, you're happier, you make more friends and you're healthier.

Lynn Hill:
"Climbing Wisdom"

A classic by any standard, Astroman (5.11c) exemplifies climbing's evolution in Yosemite and elsewhere. Warren Harding and Chuck Pratt used more than 200 pieces of direct aid on its 1,100 overhanging feet during their 1959 first ascent, an impressive and hard-fought achievement. But when John Bachar, Ron Kauk and John Long climbed the intensely demanding 12-pitch route on Washington Column entirely without aid in 1975, they shattered perceptions of what was possible in the vertical world. Astroman still ranks among Yosemite's most challenging free climbs due to its great sustained difficulty and unnerving exposure.

Attesting to that is Lynn Hill, no stranger to redefining the possible. The perennial competition champion became the first woman to climb Midnight Lightning and to free climb the West Face of Leaning Tower. Above all her free ascent of The Nose, unprecedented for both women and men, made her name widely known even outside climbing circles. For a step in her evolution, Hill credits a daunting effort on Astroman in September of 1983. As she climbed with her boyfriend, circumstances required the 22-year-old to lead the intimidating route ill-equipped and in darkness.

Yosemite is one of the most spectacular, demanding and humbling places I've ever climbed. You have to have certain epic experiences there to really learn what you're doing. Climbing Astroman was one of those times for me. Some of my friends like John Long and Ron Kauk had climbed it and talked to me about it. That climb is a legend and famous even all the way out in The Gunks, where my then-boyfriend grew up climbing. He was a fabulous 5.12

climber and always good at knowing the reputations of climbs, but in The Gunks the rock is so completely different. You hardly ever have to jam and you don't need big cams. So he didn't realize that he didn't have the background for the route.

We set out in sketchy weather. It looked like it could sprinkle but not too soon, so we decided to go for it. We'd already climbed the first few pitches when I realized we didn't have a full gear rack. My boyfriend was nine years older than me and at that age I wasn't used to being the one in charge. I was always the youngest in the group, tagging along. I didn't study the guidebook or pick out our routes or the gear. This time, it turns out we only had a couple of cams that were the right size and I realized we were going to have to run it out a lot.

When we got to the Harding Slot, it was his turn to lead. He didn't know how to jam it and the crack spit him out. He got claustrophobic and couldn't stand it so he came down. He also complained of pain from his tendinitis. "You lead," he said. So I took that pitch and then I just kept leading the pitches above that. I had to do some tricky balancing moves on some edges, pretty continuous laybacking, jamming and placing gear. It's always more difficult when you have to stop to place pro. The section between the Harding Slot and Changing Corners is probably the crux. There's a corner where you must transition from laybacking on one side of the arête to the other. We were supposed to trade leads but I was faster and we had to hurry because of darkness and the threat of rain; we hadn't brought any rain gear or bivvy gear.

And so there I was, exhausted on the last pitch in complete darkness. We didn't have headlamps, of course. It was really hard to see where to go or how to place any gear. I had to feel by hand the shape of the crack. I climbed it again later and even in daylight it's hard to find that line. It's not easy to protect in any case, which is why it gets scary rating, R. When I could use protection, the placements were so bad that I considered them pieces of decoration rather than security. I was so nervous, not only because it was run out and hard climbing. It was also over a ledge where a fall could cause a bad injury. "Don't fall" was the theme in those days. That's where I learned that first rule of climbing wisdom.

Astroman on Washington Column

When we arrived at the top it started to sprinkle. Without head-lamps, it was too dark to hike down. So we found an overhanging rock for shelter from the rain. We didn't bring much for warmth. He had an Anorack jacket and I had a cotton sweatshirt. We wrapped our rope around us. No food and no water. We'd only brought one li-ter of water for the day and I didn't get much of that. I got so desper-ate that by the following morning, I tried to sip running water on the rock face during our descent. We got down safe but I ended up get-ting a very painful bladder infection due to the lack of water. Then I had to figure out how to get medicine for that because it wasn't like I had access to a doctor.

I don't think we could have retreated. That would have been complicated. We had only one rope and we would have had to leave behind a lot of gear, which I couldn't afford. I was a dirtbag climber and didn't have rich parents to pay my way. So in a tough spot, my inclination was to figure out how to make due and get to the top.

The whole trip was epic on many levels. The climb was definitely more difficult than I had imagined. Yosemite climbs like that can be very sustained, with one pitch of 5.10 or 5.11 after another. Some-times the ratings seem lower than the actual difficulty. Then there's a more personal side of the story. He and I were moving in together. The fact that I had to kind of take over and do the hardest leading bruised his ego. So he was embarrassed and he had to deal with that. Climbing really is a good test for a partnership and that should have been a telltale sign of the future. He ended up breaking up with me and I had to find another place to live, though today we're on friendly terms.

Obviously I learned to be prepared with enough equipment, food, water and warmth needed for a long climb like that. I would bring more cams and locking carabiners. When I don't have enough biners, it becomes either more dangerous or takes extra time to pro-tect adequately. Be organized and know what you're getting into. Ask questions of people who have done the route, somebody who has the intent to give you the correct information and not someone trying to sandbag you. Just come ready. I was young and not yet ac-customed to taking more responsibility. That climb was my initiation from trusting without knowing and not being really critical to getting more organized and involved in every decision about a climb.

Watch out for ego. That's a lesson that gets relearned all the time. Let's just say it hasn't always been easy in my position. Boys really don't like it when girls do something better than them. There's no logical reason, but they always feel like they should be better at everything. Guys don't like to admit that they chickened out or couldn't do it. Take responsibility for your mistakes. Sort out your motivations for doing things and keep desires in balance and perspective. Don't set unrealistic expectations. It's more fun to choose climbs that are not so stressful. Have fun!

Hans Florine:
"Sandbag Situation"

Those familiar with the exploits of Hans Florine may not recognize him from this account of his first El Capitan ascent. As a big wall novice, he bore little resemblance to the speed climber who would one day fly 3,000 feet up The Nose in 2 hours and 37 minutes, besting the 1958 first ascent time by more than 46 days. Few enthusiasts could dream of matching such a feat, but countless others have shared the unpleasant "sandbag" experience of a surprisingly difficult challenge in the outdoors.

Florine often shook his head and chuckled at himself while recalling his climb on the formidable Salathé Wall (5.13b/A2) with partner Winston Warme in July of 1986. Struggling through 35 pitches over three days in stifling heat with insufficient food and water gave the 22-year-old abundant motivation to pioneer the practice of speed climbing in the future.

My visits to Yosemite used to be about finding the rock that was closest to the car door, going out to do one pitch, and then coming down. Frankly, I always thought big wall climbing was something I would never do. I would see people in El Cap Meadow with these huge haul bags on their backs. Stories were horrendous of classic old beatnik climbers in blue jean cutoffs who set off with a couple of cans of soup and trail mix to eat for five days. It can sound kind of adventurous, but to me it wasn't that appealing, so I wasn't psyched to do it.

But a friend of my sister was really motivated. Winston Warme was a couple of years older than me and a Green Beret. He provided the confidence, though he had never done a big wall either. I was climbing 5.10s then, which was good in the mid-80s when sport climbing hadn't really proliferated yet. But we were pretty ignorant of how to go up more than one or two pitches. At least I was.

You hear that Salathé Wall is the greatest rock route in the world. It may also have been that The Nose was crowded. The routes are only about 70 feet apart where they start. We knew it had big ledges on it, and we didn't have a portaledge. So we figured the Salathé was a good choice.

Our plan was to climb two long days and sleep one night on it. As ignorant as we were, we calculated two liters per person per day, which is not very much. Now I calculate a gallon per person per day. We had a green army duffle bag from a surplus store and two sleeping bags which we actually never got out, since we were never on a big ledge when we slept. We wore terrible clothes by today's standards. Painters' pants were in style then. I had a pair of karate pants. We were in all cotton, or as we now call it, death cloth.

We brought three cams of each size. You hear about the Salathé having all this wide stuff. I was terrified that we were going to run into trouble with that. Winston figured we'd get through it somehow. We even brought some pitons and a hammer, though I'm sure we never used them; there's another ten pounds of gear we didn't need. Nowadays I'm really big on studying the topo map and trying to top out having used every piece on the rack. But back then, we said, "Let's bring the kitchen sink. We'll find a use for it. Nothing's going to stop us!"

The first day had a lot of open face climbing and thin cracks. Both of us seemed pretty comfortable on that. We didn't free climb it, but we moved pretty well. At Heart Ledge, a lot of people send ropes down to the ground, go down for a day or two, and then send their route. But we thought we'd be bold and go all the way to El Cap Spire to bivvy, because we knew there were big ledges there. Never mind that it was another eight pitches above Heart Ledge! We were just totally clueless. Instead of asking, "Can we make it there?" we just said, "We're going to make it there."

Before we reached Mammoth Terraces, we came to The Half Dollar, this big awkward chimney that's only rated 5.8. But that's a clas-

Salathé Wall on El Capitan

sic Yosemite sandbag situation. You get in this thing, it's hot and the granite is really smooth and greasy. Elbows on one side, hands on the other, everything is slippery and you're trying to wedge up this open flare. You're climbing up a funnel that's facing down. Neither of us had ever done anything like that on granite. I hadn't done it anywhere. It was super scary, 700 feet up, in a funnel opening at your feet outwards. You try to reach back as it gets thinner and thinner, but your head stops you from reaching far enough in to place protection. Terrifying, and little did we know, that was just the warmup for the horrifying Ear, the worst open funnel pitch still higher up on the route.

We had heard that was coming, and we were a little bit intimidated there, looking up at The Ear, and saying, "Oh my God, if this is worse than The Half Dollar, we're in big trouble." So I just put Winston on that pitch, though in those situations you almost don't want to be the second, because the leader makes so much noise on the lead, whining and whatever. Then of course your fears are confirmed by the leader's moans and you're even more terrified to follow up.

The hardest pitch on the whole route was number 18, which is 5.13a or A2. I don't know why I got put on this hard aid lead. Neither of us was really the better partner. We were both just clueless and willing. It went dark when I was halfway up this pitch. We didn't bring headlamps, and I didn't have the skills to be tinkering in the dark. So it was terrifying, and really hard, and then when night fell on it, it seemed like the extra straw that broke the back. "Lower me down, lower me down!" I said. I lowered down to the ledge above the Ear where Winston was. It was 9 or 10 p.m. and we couldn't really do anything because it was dark. So we sat there on this sloping 45-degree ledge, shifting our buns every once in a while, trying to wrap slings underneath our legs. It was just sloping enough that we could never get comfortable. I'd doze for five or ten minutes and then my leg would fall asleep and wake me up in total pain.

Little did I know that where I left gear in and lowered back down to the sloping ledge, I was only two gear placements from a ledge I could have reached by struggling a little longer. If I had just fought for 30 more minutes in the dark, we would have been on a ledge all night. That really dampened our spirits, at least mine. I was so cranky and exhausted from struggling to sleep all night.

A pitch below The Block always has this black vegetation on it. A couple of times, moss came down into my face while Winston was leading. You think you're up on this big clean granite wall and all is going well, but it's pretty scary when you're hot and sweaty with dirt and moss coming down on you.

By the second night, we were supposed to be back on the ground sleeping in our tent at Camp 4. But we had only made it to this classic roof crack in the middle of a huge headwall, the other 5.13a pitch that you have to do. We got stuck right in the middle of the headwall, the most overhanging place on the whole route. So we lowered two rope lengths down to the Sous le Toit ledge. There was enough room for both of us to kind of spoon there with our knees hanging off the edge. We couldn't rappel down to a bigger ledge because we didn't have enough rope, and we didn't have the knowledge or the desire to abandon our high point and go down there. That would have killed us. At that point we ate the last of our food, and we still didn't know if we were going to make the last three or four pitches, or go down. So it was a double misery hit.

We ran out of water two or three pitches from the top, and we needed really sparse rationing to make it go that far. I wish when we topped out on the level ground, it could have been this thing where we hugged each other and cheered, but that wasn't it. I don't remember a lot of jubilation, because it was miserably hot and we didn't have water. Now I know that when you top out on El Cap, you can look underneath the bushes and trees along the top and often find water. But I didn't know that then, so we started the death march down the East Ledges. As worn as that trail is now, I don't know how we found it or how we made it back down to the Manure Pile Buttress area. Now that I've done the descent 140 times, it's easy. But then it felt like 120 degrees, we had all these leaves and grit and dirt on us and we still had to carry a haul bag full of stuff.

We must have looked pretty terrible when we got to El Cap Meadow. I was really thin and my cheeks were sucked in. My sister and my mom were there. There was a look on my mom's face like, "Oh God, my son is a walking skeleton." She shuddered and her eyes got really big when I came out of the woods. I remember plopping down on the lawn chair, having a nice big deli sandwich, water and juice. The refueling was a notable good time.

When you're in your 20s, you don't know you're supposed to stop when you're under that much duress. Adventure climbers seem to do a little better in their 30s, 40s and 50s, partly because you learn your body a little bit better. You know you've got to eat something before you're hungry. That's one of my big things: keep the bonk off! We were just bonking all over the place on this route. I got on a scale and was super surprised I lost 15 pounds.

The Salathé was definitely an adventure where the outcome was not known ahead of time. It was very, very unsure that we would even live through it, let alone get to the top. We got through with perseverance and youthful exuberance. We would have been far better if we'd just asked somebody, "Hey, what should we look for on the route?" It's smart to ask those who have gone before you. You don't need to worry about losing the adventure by asking for advice. There will still be plenty of adventure out there.

I had lots of thoughts like, "I'm never going to do this again!" I thought it was a pretty good bet I'd never climb El Cap again, because I thought that was the only style you could do El Cap. I didn't know it was possible to do it any other way. But I realize the suffering on this route was the impetus for all the light and fast speed climbing I did later on.

I went back to the Salathé four years later and we did the whole route in 12 hours. I had learned a ton from the first time to the second time. I remember getting back to the meadow in the light and thinking, "Wow, the last time I did this, I slept right there on The Ear!" After that I did it in seven hours flat. That's a wild juxtaposition, to know that something is hard or even impossible at first, and then it's easy. A lot of things are that way.

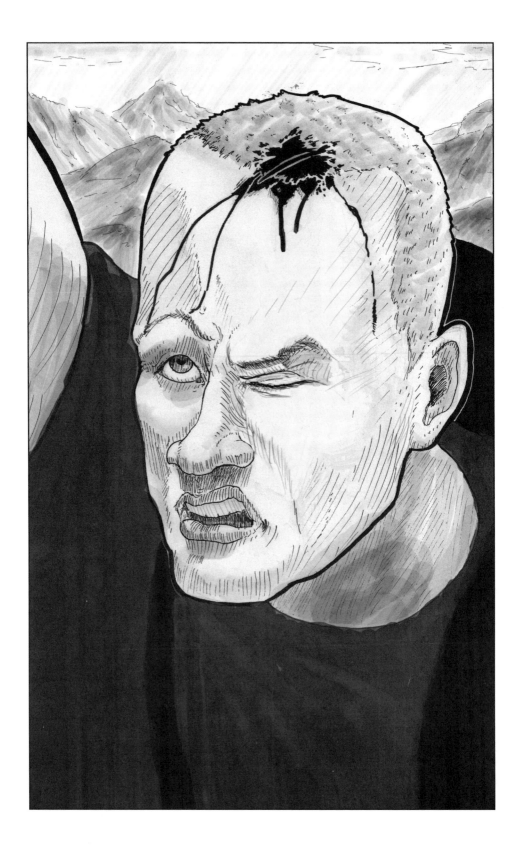

Doug Englekirk:
"The Lord Watches Over Me"

While Yosemite attracts climbers from around the world, El Capitan attracts more of their attention than any other part of Yosemite. Between its grand faces of sculpted granite and more than 70 routes, one easily sees why. Ascending the mountain even once highlights the careers of many climbers. Countless dramatic tales surrounding the mountain add to its mystique and magnetism.

Count Doug Englekirk among those who have felt the pull. A three-time national climbing champion, he's one of few to climb Yosemite 5.13s like Quantum Mechanic, Book of Hate and the West Face of Leaning Tower. Elsewhere Englekirk topped challenges as hard as 5.14b. Before becoming a rock star, however, he learned the ropes on The Captain. Setting a goal in 1986 to solo an El Cap route, the 24-year-old tied himself in for three daring adventures in the next four years that would hone his world-class ability and tenacity.

I'd been climbing for several years but I wasn't that experienced with aid climbing yet. With a partner, I'd done some walls like The Nose, Triple Direct and the Regular Route of Half Dome, but nothing really difficult. I always thought it would be cool to solo an El Cap route. That sounded like a worthy challenge.

Dihedral Wall (5.9/A3+, 27 pitches) was the route I chose. It's pretty straightforward with good cracks. I liked the sweeping right-facing corners that go up it most of the way. I wasn't thinking of free climbing. I thought I'd be lucky to aid climb something like that. The best way to place aid is to bounce on it a few times and test it with some body weight to make sure it's going to hold you, but my idea at the time was to put a piece in and ease all my weight onto it slowly. That's a little faster but the problem is that if the placement isn't strong enough to hold you, it pops out and you fall with momentum onto the lower gear. Then you can rip through several pieces in a zipper fall. That's what happened to me on the fourth pitch. My piece blew, I ripped out four more pieces and fell 40 feet. When I came to a stop, I was spinning in the air upside down.

I wasn't hurt, though, so I pulled myself up and kept climbing. When I fell again, only 20 feet this time, the rope wrapped around my wrist and twisted it. I spent the night on a ledge hoping it would feel better, but in the morning my wrist was sore and swollen and I had to rappel. Rather than dropping my heavy pitons and gear, I put everything on my back. Rappelling one-handed through a lot of hanging belays was scary, hard and fairly painful but eventually I got down.

After I failed on that, I thought, "Well, maybe I should try something harder next time." My first hard aid route was the second ascent of El Cap's Space (5.10/A4+, 28 pitches) with Randy Leavitt. On that climb I'd learned about making difficult aid placements. After that I felt ready to try a harder aid solo. Jolly Roger (5.10/A5, 23 pitches) was way harder than Dihedral Wall, like night and day. The route had only been climbed once and attempted a few other times. One climber suffered a 120-foot fall on it and bailed. Another suffered a 200-foot fall and bailed. No one had soloed it. It may have been foolhardy but I thought it was worth a try.

I showed up in El Cap Meadow the next year, racked up my stuff and got started. Jolly Roger follows a line back and forth beneath The Heart. There's pretty hard aid climbing and a lot of hooking. On my third day I reached a pretty good ledge below The Heart. Those other climbers took their falls on the next pitch from there, I'd heard. You have to leave this ledge, free climb out left past a pillar, clip a bolt, rappel down 70 feet and then pendulum over to the left. From there you ascend this featured granite face with some bowls and bulges until you're about 100 feet above that bolt. There's a last 5.8 mantle move before you get any protection. I did all this, reached the mantle and could see my next bolt above.

Dihedral Wall (left), Jolly Roger (center) and The Nose (right) on El Capitan

Then I discovered there was a little stream of water going right over the mantle move you have to do. That's the last thing you want when you're run out so far and looking at a 200-foot fall. But I had my aid gear with me, so I pulled out a big fish hook that I placed on a little ledge. I stood as high as I could on it but couldn't reach the bolt. I stepped back down and placed another hook on an edge a little bit higher. That one didn't seem quite so good, so I bounced on it a little to test it. Under my weight the hook sprang off the edge and hit me in the head. This is before I got in the habit of wearing a helmet. The hook gashed my forehead and I started bleeding pretty good. And I was still 100 feet up and I still had to do this move!

Finally I ended up taking a little sling and attaching it to the first, stronger fish hook so I could get a higher foothold. From that I was able to stand higher, step onto the next ledge and reach that bolt. By then it was getting late in the afternoon so I rappelled from that bolt back down to the ledge with my gear. I couldn't really tell how badly cut I was. I decided to spend the night and see how I felt in the morning.

Before dawn, some guys came by ascending fixed lines to the Heart Ledges.

"How does my head look?" I asked one of them.

"You may need stitches, but it's probably too late for that now," he answered.

"All right, cool," I said. "I'll keep going."

So I jumared back up to my high point and started again on the aid climbing, which involved going up an expanding flake and doing some hook moves past that. I got to The Heart and continued from there for a couple of days. Solo aid climbing goes fairly slowly.

At the Golden Doubloon, the wall becomes a totally blank rock with no seam for protection or hook placements. I saw a ledge high above and I tried throwing a hook to snag it, but that didn't work. The only thing I found to use was a slot in the rock the size of a dime on its edge. So I took a little copperhead and tried to smash it down with my hammer. That was the only way I could see to go on. I stood on this thing and bounced a few times to test it. Then the piece popped off and hit me in the head! It was a different spot than before but my forehead started bleeding again.

"Oh man, this is ridiculous," I thought. So I rappelled back down to Mammoth Terraces, where I left my haul bag, and then rapped from there to the ground. I wanted to find a helmet to borrow so I could go back up and keep climbing. Back then the idea of buying a helmet was silly to me. I did find a helmet which belonged to a guy keen on doing The Shield (5.9/A3+, 29 pitches). He didn't look like he had the experience to do a wall that hard, though, so I ended up going along with him and I didn't finish Jolly Roger.

I still wanted to solo an El Cap route and two years later I got the idea to climb The Nose (5.13b/A2, 34 pitches) in 24 hours, which no solo climber had done. That's more a test of endurance than a hard aid challenge. I'd heard that Steve Schneider had tried it the year before. He reached Camp 6 but had gotten tired, spent the night there and topped out the next day. So I decided to try it on the longest day of the year under a full moon when everything seemed right for an attempt.

When most people try a hard climb in a 24-hour period, they start around 7 p.m. To me, the time to start was midnight. I drove into the valley that morning and got my stuff ready. I tried to nap but I was too excited and hyped up to sleep. So I was basically up all day. That night I wandered to the base and started soloing.

I cruised along, not going real fast but doing okay, I thought. I got to Camp 5 the next afternoon. By then I'd been up 40 straight hours. I was getting pretty tired and thirsty. My water was running low. I probably wasn't as fit as I could have been. I'd been doing pull-ups but I hadn't been climbing a bunch of walls at the time.

At about 7 p.m., I passed a guy and his girlfriend getting set to bivvy for the night at Camp 5. While we talked I told them I was trying to solo The Nose in a day.

"That's great," the guy said. "Steve Schneider did that three days ago!"

I could hardly believe it. I've always been competitive, I had wanted to be the first and that news really took the wind out of my sails.

"So what are you going to do?" the guy asked.

"Keep going," I said.

I got to Camp Six and found a little water to drink. I rested about

15 minutes. Then I kept going and topped out at 12:30 a.m. I think I could have made it by midnight if I'd hurried, but Steve had already done it and I just thought "Whatever." I was still happy I soloed an El Cap route in only a little more than a day.

By the time I got my stuff sorted out, it was 1:30 in the morning. I'd been up 42 hours and I tried to rest, though I kept shivering in the cold and couldn't sleep. I decided to hike back down. Once I descended the East Ledges, it was 7 a.m. I started to drive to Crane Flat. But I fell asleep at the wheel and rolled my truck into a ditch.

I hit my head, again, on the windshield this time. Nobody else saw the accident and the truck was totaled so I had to climb out of the ditch and flag down a car. An ambulance took me back to the valley. I was so tired that I dozed off waiting for the doctor to stitch me up. I finally got to sleep after 56 hours. If I had that one to do over, I'd probably start first thing in the morning and sleep in the woods for a while after finishing. Thankfully I'm hardheaded and the Lord watches over me.

I think I learned about the importance of being able to keep your calm, especially when I was bleeding in that situation 100 feet run out and having to do that wet 5.8 move. It's important to not panic. I learned to wear a helmet when you're doing hard aid climbing, though shortly after that I got more into sport climbing. I like the hard physical challenge of free climbing without all the suffering that goes with wall climbing.

For me life is about adventure. I tend to bite off more than I can chew sometimes but I like to push myself to see what I can do. Even though I wasn't totally successful on some of those climbs, the experiences were worth it in their own right.

Steve Schneider:
"If God had Meant for Man to Fly"

Steve Schneider has no shortage of Yosemite adventures to share. Nick-named "Shipoopoi" after one of his favorite Tuolumne routes, the veteran climber became the first to solo El Capitan's Nose and Salathé Wall, both in a single day. By scaling Freerider at age 45, he became the oldest athlete to free climb an El Cap route. And he spent ten years on Yosemite's elite search and rescue team.

Such achievements put Schneider in rare company, but equally uncommon is his light heart that lets him smile and laugh through the story of a bone-breaking paragliding accident. Shipoopoi's ill-fated flight near the park's eastern border occurred in 1987, when he was 27.

I won my paraglider from the Wild Things climbing company. They were having a competition for the raddest climber of the year, and I'd climbed some hard things and had a pretty good ré-sumé. At first they were kind of secretive about it: "We have an interesting descent device for you." I thought they would give me some sort of super rappel device. Instead I got the paraglider. I hadn't used one before but it sounded like major booty for me. I was ready to snag it up whatever it was.

With a paraglider, you can hike up a hill or a peak and then fly off. There was the potential to do some great linkups in Yosemite, like climb Half Dome, fly down to the valley, bike to El Cap, climb that and call it a day. Except that it's illegal in Yosemite. The rangers weren't into it and they were busting everyone.

We went out to Bishop and flew off chossy rubble piles into the wind, sometimes with bloody results. This one guy tried it and was running to take off. The teacher John was yelling, "Go! Go! Go!" The guy stopped, pulled the wing down and landed in some shale that cut his hands up. He thought John was saying, "No! No! No!" There were a lot of accidents when those things first came out and everyone was getting hurt. They didn't have the designs of today and the instruction wasn't so good. My lessons sucked!

Tioga Peak is right outside the park. Apparently it wasn't illegal to jump off that peak, even though it's within spitting distance of Yosemite. So I didn't have to face any fines for flying off it. I may be blonde but I'm not stupid! It took a couple of hours to hike up Tioga Peak, which is a total rubble pile of chossy, volcanic rock. There's a nice big meadow right in front of the Junction campground there. I thought it would be pretty hard to miss the meadow. I had a girlfriend Shira who was my ground team waiting for me there, and I had instructed her to throw some dust in the air so I could see the wind direction. You want to land going into the wind to reduce your speed.

To set up, you lay out the chute and clip into the harness which connects to the glider with all these little strings. It's nice to have the wind coming up the hillside, which should be steep and clear. Then you run down as fast as you can until your legs are treading air.

This day it was windy and I was getting frustrated because I was having a hard time getting my chute managed. The wind was blowing it around and I was repeatedly getting knocked off my launch spot. I should have just packed it in. Instead, I stuck with it and finally got a launch. But instead of running down and going forward like usual, I launched and got taken vertically straight up into the air. I didn't know the wind was going to affect me like it did. I kind of hovered and occasionally would rise. I tried to point down to go to the meadow, but all I did was go up and up, slowly at first and then faster. We didn't know much about altitude control in those days, except you knew you were going down at some point. This was before people were really soaring with it, working hillsides and having multi-hour flights.

I'm 200 feet above my launch point on the mountain. Then there's another big gust. Whoosh! Instantly I go up another 100 feet. I realize I'm in an updraft, riding these strong mountain currents launching me up. Seven, eight, nine minutes go by, and finally I'm about 500 feet above my launch point and getting blown downwind away from the meadow. So I'm thinking, "Okay, I can't make my landing." I look around and in the other direction I see another meadow way down in Tioga Canyon. I think I can make that one. So I turned around 180 degrees, and as soon as I did that, I started dropping and roaring fast down the canyon.

I'm just hauling ass, 30 miles per hour down the canyon and dropping like a bat out of hell. I'm coming down really freaking quick. I'm hoping that I'm going to have enough altitude to reach the meadow, and I wanted to fully play that out, because it looked like if I could get there I could set down without hitting any trees or obstructions. But after a minute, it's obvious that I'm not going to make it. "Okay, bummer!" I've gotta do something else. I decided to make a turn and tried to head into the wind to make a landing somewhere else.

Shira was apparently still throwing sand in the air as I disappeared behind the mountain, even though I was miles away and could barely see the meadow, let alone the sand!

During my 14-minute flight, I was not scared. I was more cool but concerned. I've been in many desperate situations before with climbing and kayaking and whatever, and up until the moment that I actually slammed into the ground, I thought I was going to miraculously escape unscathed.

There's this rocky hillside under me and in the middle of my turn, I hit that thing. I had almost turned upwind so I was just about neutral with my groundspeed, but I was dropping too fast out of the sky. If I had another 30 or 40 feet, I could have made a decent landing. As it was, it was like jumping off a 30-foot cliff onto a rocky hillside with brush and granite boulders. Luckily, my head was the last thing that hit, although I fully crumpled to the ground.

I did a self-evaluation and basically knew that I had possible ankle and lower leg damage from my impact, but my head and spine and neck were okay. So I got on my knee pads and started a pretty comfortable crawl toward the road. I didn't realize that a lot of people had seen me and that a rescue had been initiated. I crawled about a half mile and was just about 200 feet from the road when rescuers looking for me came through the trees. I had full Kaiser health insurance, and I knew I was going to go way over my $100 deductible, so I was able to casually accept the ambulance ride to the hospital in Mammoth.

I think it's everyone's right to have one rescue if you've messed up your body in some way and you need help. Try not to have a second one. But I really don't count this as a rescue because I was pretty much rescuing myself. So I've still got mine saved up for when I really need it.

I broke one ankle and sprained the other, which was sore for a few days. My fibula was broken. The tibia was okay. So it was not too dangerous of a leg break. For the ankle, the doctor had to go in there and extract a few fragments. As they wheeled me into the operation room, I turned to Shira and calmly said in the bravery of anesthetic, "Don't worry, KAREN, it's going to be all right." Karen had been my last girlfriend! The nurse, catching the name swap, turned compassionately to Shira and said "It's okay, honey, people get pretty messed up on these drugs."

The worst pain of the whole thing was when the doctor went to reset the bones. Even though I had some anesthesia, shifting my bones back into place hurt to all hell. The nurse gave me a hard time about being a baby. I was ready to destroy her but I couldn't reach over there to actually do it. But I showed her, by all the stuff I did later. Three El Cap routes in a day, babe! In fact, about seven months after my accident and subsequent operations, I raced my anesthesiologist in the Mammoth Mountain Marathon. We battled with lead changes for the last 20 minutes of the race. He beat me, but he didn't have a broken freaking ankle!

That's the story of the first descent of Lee Vining Canyon, and one of the first paragliding crashes in California. The paragliding fad sort of came and went. It never became the tool of choice for climbers trying to climb and descend fast, because BASE jumping is more efficient, I believe. I never launched and flew again, and now I can't find the paraglider, which is probably good.

I learned that I'm a tough mofo and I can really take some pain, damn it! And I also learned the same thing the bad guys in a James Bond movie said when they blew up a helicopter: "If God had meant for man to fly, he would have given him wings."

Scott Cosgrove: "Affliction"

A thin line separates passion and obsession and those who cross it risk serious consequences. Yet only a seemingly superhuman drive permits some outdoors enthusiasts to accomplish their most mind-boggling feats. Scott Cosgrove and Walt Shipley proved as much as they pioneered a daring climb on Higher Cathedral Rock in July of 1990. The virgin route they attempted presented the pair with challenges even greater than its formidable 5.12 climbing difficulty.

Cosgrove, then just 21, served with the veteran Shipley on Yosemite's search and rescue team. "Coz" had already achieved first free ascents of Half Dome's Southern Belle and Machine Gun, a 5.13c rock face which was the park's hardest climb for years. But none of his previous efforts involved the combined physical and mental tenacity required on the 1,500-foot terror which the duo aptly named The Affliction.

W hen I climbed a first ascent of Power Point with Werner Braun on Higher Cathedral Rock, I looked around a corner and saw a hairline crack going across the north face. It was a big, shady, intimidating line that comes right out of a catwalk gully. I went to check it out from the ground and saw it was a gigantic, right-facing corner. Nobody had ever climbed it before and I showed it to Walt Shipley, who was looking to do a first free ascent. He got excited and we decided to go for it.

Walt was a famous, well-liked climber and something of a mentor. When I moved to Yosemite, I was 19 years old and he was about 32. He was a really bright guy, a former Lockheed engineer and super-talented at everything from free climbing to direct aid to ice climbing. He was also totally crazy.

We had gone climbing together before. I wasn't quite the wall climber he was. I was just starting out when we tried to do Mescalito on El Cap. I decided to bail and he was frustrated and disappointed in me. I was really good at first free ascents, though. I wanted to impress Walt by doing this climb with him, but I don't know if I did that. He was a hard guy to impress.

The route looks spectacular from the ground and I was hoping it would be really good, but there's a reason no one had ever climbed there before. That's because it's loose and dark on one of these Yosemite faces that almost never sees sun. When we got up there we found it wasn't the best rock, but we decided to go ahead anyway. Walt said, "Let's do it in a day." I didn't want to say that we couldn't do it in a day. So we just took a minimal amount of gear, food and water for the first ascent. A lot of crazy things went on and we had to fight for every inch up there.

We started heading up and turned a corner onto the north face. We get to the face and there's a gigantic drop-off into a gully. We started climbing up this corner and it turned out to be just nasty, vegetated and dirty with gigantic loose blocks, though the climbing itself was generally okay. Walt led the first pitch and he actually drilled a bolt straight away to protect a 5.12 face move. Then there was a really scary 5.11 section.

"Coz, this thing sucks," Walt shouted. "But it's just right for us. Nobody else will ever do it!"

The next pitch was the scariest thing I've ever seen in my life. Four gigantic flakes, 30 feet by 20 feet and three feet thick, sit on top of each other with no visible attachment to the wall whatsoever. We're two pitches from the start but way above the gully and thousands of feet off the ground. In my head a voice says "I don't want to do this!" But I also didn't want to let Walt down. That turned out to be the bigger priority.

It felt really wrong, but I started leading. When I got to the first flake, it was even worse than I thought. I compensated by putting a bunch of gear in behind it, even though the gear could pull the flake from the wall. Walt commented that he'd never seen me put so much

The Affliction on Higher Cathedral Rock

gear onto one pitch, but the climb was 5.11c and loose and I was terrified.

After I get on top of the third flake, I get back into the corner we saw from the ground and we're back to good pro again. I still can't believe how crazy that pitch was, but the pitch after that was even crazier. Walt led a super-overhanging flake with hard stemming and really sporadic pro. He'd go 25 feet, place a cam, climb another 25 feet and place another one, all on solid 5.11c. He only placed five pieces on the entire pitch. That was the epitome of Walt's climbing ability and style. With his engineering mind, he could always find the best protection, and he was crazy enough to totally rely on it.

Our last pitch that day took us to a big ledge. To get there, I had to lead desperately loose 5.11c. Walt was really impressed when he got to the ledge but it was clear we weren't going to top out that day.

"You know Scott, we've got enough food and water. Let's just sleep here tonight," Walt says. I think, "We don't have any bivvy gear." But I don't want to let him down, so I agreed.

We wanted to let our girlfriends know we were okay and we saw these guys descending from the East Buttress of Middle Cathedral. So Walt dropped rocks down the gully to get their attention. They didn't notice right away and there was no way the rock would hit them, so Walt finally threw a gigantic rock that made a huge explosion.

"What the hell!" they yell.

We tell them, "Hey, we're Walt and Scott. Please go tell our girlfriends in Camp 4 that we're okay and sleeping on this rock tonight."

They probably worried we'd throw more rocks and kill them and didn't want to go down the gully after that. Walt was a nut job and thought it was funny to throw bigger and bigger rocks. They said "Whatever" and they actually did find our girlfriends. Then they said to them, "Your boyfriends are screwed up! What did you do to them?"

That was the coldest night recorded that spring and we started a little fire on our ledge. Walt started snuggling up to me to keep warm. I wasn't going for that and I slept on the other side of the fire. I remember thinking, "I don't want to be here, but I don't want Walt to think I'm a wimp." We toughed out the night.

In the morning we tried to traverse past a couple of bolts. Walt tried to climb past them and place a third bolt but had trouble doing that without hanging on the bolts that were already there.

"Walt, you're not strong enough. You need to lock off on the bolt and lean out," I said.

"I'm not strong enough? You arrogant son of a bitch!" He just lost it and started screaming and going off on me.

"Sorry Walt, I didn't mean it that way!" This was my worst nightmare. Here I was trying to impress him and instead I get him mad at me.

"I'm not good enough?" he says. "This climb sucks. We're going down!"

We rappelled, hiked down and got back that afternoon, totally wasted. We both swore we weren't going to have anything to do with the climb again.

Then a day went by and I went over to his van.

"Don't say it!" he said.

But I did anyway. "I want to go back."

"So do I," he said.

So we went back up there again with the same plan: crank to the top in one day. We got back to our ledge where we bivvied before. Walt leads the next pitch again and this time he clips the second bolt and swings over from it into a crack system. I followed and now it's my lead in a gigantic off-width corner. I got into this thing and it's so hard I almost die. I'd been climbing in Colorado where the rock is totally different and I can't get up. So Walt takes over and leads beautifully to the top of that stellar off-width pitch.

I lead the pitch after that and get to another giant loose block, like the ones below only way worse. I touch it with my finger and the whole thing moves. This block is 60 feet high and right above our ledge. The whole geology up there is loose and this flake could peel away like a giant onion at any minute. I won't climb it. Walt thinks I'm being a wimp, but then he looks at it and he won't do it either. We decide to bail again.

He lowered me a ways and I clipped into a bolt. I wanted to add another bolt to rappel from there. "Walt, send me down the bolt kit," I said.

"No! We're not adding a bolt."

He was mad about his girlfriend running around with some other guy and wanted to get down in a hurry. So he takes me off belay, rappels down to me and clips right into my carabiner in the bolt. Now we're both hanging from a single quarter-inch bolt because he's too pissed off to add another one! He raps off the bolt, swings around at the bottom of the rope and jumps onto a ledge. I had to follow him. I'm the young protégé and I don't want to bug him too much, but I couldn't believe he did that. We're fighting and pissed off all the way back to camp, and we swear we're never going back up there again.

But the next day, I go back to his van.

"Don't even say it!" he said.

"I want to go back," I said.

"Me too," he said.

First we had to figure out how to get past the flake. We hiked to the top and I rapped down three pitches, leaving Walt at the summit. I just put my hand on it and this whole 60-foot pillar flies off. It was like kicking a Greyhound bus off the wall. Slowly it turns over and over, hits the Middle Cathedral catwalk and explodes. The shit we were doing for this climb just kept getting more insane.

As we hiked the approach again, Walt stopped in the talus and looked at me.

"What's wrong with you, Coz?"

"What do you mean?" I said.

"You've got a great girlfriend. You're one of the best climbers in the valley. But you're not happy down on the ground. You're only happy when you're up here climbing."

"What are you talking about?"

"You have an affliction."

That's why we called it The Affliction. Maybe he was right, because no matter what happened to us, we kept throwing ourselves back up there.

We start again and we get back to that part where the block used to be. There's a gigantic right-facing corner followed by a huge crack. Walt pulls into this 5.11c off-width fist jam. Then I lead a 5.11a corner and I had to belay him on two small stoppers, not even close to what you want for an anchor. He gets up to me and sees the meager pro and he just goes postal.

"You idiot! We could die, Coz!" This from the guy who rapped off one bolt!

He leads a hard 5.11c fist jam pitch past this roof that hangs over the entire valley. I follow that and lead the last pitch. Finally we top out.

It felt really good but also irresponsible, like if you go to Vegas for the weekend, party too hard and say, "Why the hell did I do that?" Between the one bolt we rapped from, the loose block we pushed off, that weak anchor I belayed from, the bivvy and all the pitches down below, it was a scary, horrible 1,500 feet. It didn't feel right to me but Walt was stoked out of his mind and really happy by contrast.

My lesson was that a commitment to a friend, even if you don't feel like following through with it, is more important than anything else. On every pitch, we were going to make it or have a bad accident. We had every reason not to go on, but I'd committed so I never backed off or told him I was scared. I'm still the same way. I really think long and hard before I agree to something because I believe in taking responsibility for my decisions.

That affliction that Walt talked about is the same feeling that all climbers have when a climb gets under their skin and they really want to do it. Walt claimed that he and I had it so bad that we just weren't right for this planet. We didn't belong. In many ways, I think he was right.

Peter Croft:
"Hunted"

*Centuries before Yosemite became an international sensation, its origi-
nal residents made their home a land of legend. According to one Indian
tale, a worm saved two wayward bear cubs atop El Capitan, leading other
grateful animals to name the mountain "Tu-tok-a-nu-la" in its honor. A different fable recounts how The Great Spirit punished a husband and wife for
quarreling in the tranquil Valley of Ahwahnee, turning them into granite
giants that were forever separated: Half Dome and Washington Column.
Another legend warns of Pohono, an evil spirit haunting Bridalveil Falls
who lures unwitting victims to a watery doom.*

*Peter Croft didn't know that tale when he roped up by the falls in the
spring of 1992, though he certainly didn't lack Yosemite expertise. In an extraordinary career featuring countless bold and breathtaking ascents, Croft
chooses as his favorite achievements his trademark link-ups of multiple long
and hard routes. The pairs of El Cap and Half Dome, Astroman and The
Rostrum, and The Nose and Salathé Wall all fell to Croft, each set on a
single astonishing day. Guiding a client up eight pitches on Bridalveil East
(5.10c) did not worry the 34-year-old guide. Before their adventure was
over, however, Pohono's icy breath left a lasting chill in both of them.*

I was guiding a client that day and he didn't want to go someplace
crowded with tons of other people. We talked over a few ideas.
Though I'd never climbed it before, I suggested Bridalveil East.
I'd heard that was a good route right by the waterfall and not terribly
hard. My client was a solid, experienced climber and I thought doing
a route of that kind of length and grade would go just fine.

We didn't begin too early as I didn't feel we needed an alpine start. The weather was perfect, the route isn't that long and the approach is pretty short. We hiked up the tourist trail to the base of the falls and got started on the crack system that leans diagonally left and up. We'd climbed a few pitches and everything was going well when the wind picked up and blew a little spray onto us. But our route took us away from the falls so I thought there shouldn't be a problem as we climbed higher.

As we kept going, the wind swept more and more super-icy water on top of us. It was starting to get pretty bad. Because the crack beneath us led down and right, we would have had to rappel right through the waterfall to retreat. So for better or worse, we were committed.

There weren't fixed anchors so I was trying to figure out belay stations as I went along. We were four pitches up when things got much worse really quickly. As I was belaying him up, suddenly the whole waterfall fell right on top of us. Beneath me the rope completely disappeared into a torrent of water.

I can't see him, I can't hear him, I'm pulling as hard as I can and I'm getting nothing. I managed to place a piece of gear above me and I cranked on the rope to pull the guy up. I even turned upside-down to push my legs against the overhanging rock as hard as I could. Nothing. It felt like the rope was stuck. Freezing water pounded down on my head. I could feel my arms and hands going numb. I was on the verge of going badly hypothermic.

When he failed to move for at least 20 minutes – it felt massively longer than that, like forever – I worried he may have drowned. I couldn't know but it was possible. What should I do? One option that came to me was to tie off the rope and free solo out of there, though it was horrible to think about leaving him behind. At what point does that become the right move? After an hour? Four hours? When it gets dark? I was supposed to be in control of the situation, but if I waited too long, then we could have both died.

During this time I could see down below families picnicking at the base of the waterfall. Kids were playing and chasing each other and their parents were laughing. Even if they saw us, none of them knew that anything was wrong. That was such a bizarre contrast.

Bridalveil East beside Bridalveil Falls

For us, it was clawing for survival, hypothermia, life and death. For them, it was "I'll have another slice of watermelon, please." We were having no picnic, that's for sure.

My brain was getting numb and I could tell I was starting to lose it. I just kept on screaming and pulling the rope. The waterfall slackened a little. Then the rope started to move the tiniest bit. Finally he climbed up to me. It turned out that he hid under an overhang when the waterfall got so heavy that he struggled to breathe. He was also fighting to get our gear back beneath the torrential downpour. I yelled at him to leave anything that didn't come out easily because that situation was no time to be cheap.

I knew I had to get us out of there as fast as possible, but the route was completely soaked. My chalk was like soggy pizza dough. From then on I didn't even look for where the route actually goes. I just started totally going for it on anything I could find. It became a 5.11 lead through an overhang without any protection but the belay, though then the climb eased off a bit. I could see easy ground above and I only had to climb a 5.8 slab to get to it. But the waterfall was still chasing us.

I reached a foothold on dry rock and I thought I'd gotten out of trouble. I stopped to chalk up, forgetting that my chalk bag was totally soaked. Then while I was trying to dry my hands, a last big gust came up and blew a big spray of water all over the rock. Instantly the slab turned glassy and slick. There was no way I could climb it then and I didn't know how long the wind would keep spraying water or when the sun would dry the rock. I knew that as the day cooled off, the winds should die down. But logic was only part of the equation because it seemed that no matter what I did, things kept going wrong. The rope trailed beneath me and draped past the overhang. My belay was more than 100 feet below. If I took a fall, it would be incredibly gigantic.

Eventually the slab did dry up, I scampered up the rock and into the forest above, tied off to a tree and brought up my partner.

"Peter, that was amazing, you got us out of that horrendous mess!" he said.

"Wait a minute, I'm the one who got us into that mess!" I said.

He saw me as the hero but I thought I'd completely screwed up. I apologized to him for placing us in a bad situation. I didn't want him thinking that I'd done everything right. All of us should recognize when we make mistakes and cause dangerous problems so that we learn from those situations.

It's also important to see actual risk as opposed to perceived risk. People drive 80 m.p.h. and tailgate each other while playing with their cell phones. That's so normal that some don't view it as dangerous until one person blows it and somebody dies. Even then, who says they won't drive in cars anymore because it's too dangerous? If you got killed in a car collision or drowned in a waterfall, it would be equally tragic, though there are far more close calls and accidents in cars than there are in climbing situations.

I've been stuck in storms and other tough spots. Usually you slow down and place more gear, but this was different and I couldn't deal with it in those types of ways. It felt like the climb sucked us in by appearing so friendly. Then it hunted us and tried to get us. I never felt that way before. Finally it let us go.

I found out afterwards that local Indians believe that waterfall is haunted. That certainly played into how I felt about it later. I'm not sure I believe in that sort of stuff, but if I'd known I might have started an hour earlier because it never hurts to stack the odds in your favor.

I thought about it a lot and it's hard to come up with anything else I should have done differently. I could have asked around or checked out the afternoon winds there the day before. We could have waited until the fall to climb there when the waterfall is smaller and warmer. Then again I never encountered anything like this before or since, so I'd say the main lesson is stuff happens.

Peter Mayfield:
"The Deeper Connection"

All who have labored through the mountains under heavy backpacks understand the appeal of traveling fast and light. However, getting by without the usual comforts like sleeping bags is easier said than done, especially deep in a Sierra Nevada winter.

Peter Mayfield made his name in climbing circles with first ascents of Half Dome's Big Chill and El Capitan's Zenyatta Mondatta, serving as Yosemite Mountaineering School's chief guide for seven years. In February of 1995, he set off alone on a trans-Sierra trek with little besides his skis and the clothes on his back. Many parties would take a week to cover his 50-mile, all-wilderness route from Badger Pass to Mammoth Lakes. Mayfield, 33, tried to cross the distance in just two days and one nearly-sleepless night, but moving quickly was not his only consideration.

One moonless night I wandered through the granite ridges and lodgepole valleys of Tuolumne without a headlamp. Relishing the sharpened senses acquired through the lack of battery-powered light, I moved through the dark woods like a deer, aware of sounds and shadows, making it through on my balance and intuitive sense of the grain of the land. As I walked, I was full of visions of lower-impact adventures. Lack of equipment would increase the texture of the experience, and gear would be replaced by skill, strength and strategy.

At that time I was really thinking about sustainability. My friends nicknamed me "Eco Pete." I was deeply affected by my awakening awareness that I care about the planet, and yet I run all over the place in my 4Runner, guiding and teaching and driving 35,000 miles a year. How do we celebrate our connection to the earth through sports like backcountry skiing and climbing, knowing that as we transport ourselves and our toys around the Sierra, we leave a large ecological footprint? Our devotional trips to the mountains degrade the very environment we have come to depend upon for our play and adventure. Our continuous shopping for the ultimate pack, ski, tent or stove feeds a system of petroleum overuse, toxic waste, landfill overflow and in some cases exploitation of third world workers.

I thought a different relationship with gear could add a new dimension to mountain adventure. I wanted to express myself in mountaineering while leaving behind the smallest possible footprint, at least where equipment is concerned. My idea was not to overcome the terrain with equipment, but to expand my abilities to deal with the terrain.

The next summer, a friend and I climbed The Nose on El Capitan in a day without Jumars or aid slings. Leading and following each pitch, we never let go of the rock to climb a rope or walk up nylon ladders and found joy in the greater continuity of movement.

That winter I tried my hand at backcountry skate skiing. I had raced seriously in the 80s, and taking it to the high Sierra combined my love of skating with my mountaineering experience.

In February of 1995, I drove into Yosemite Valley over Crane Flat on the kind of clear day when you can see your favorite peaks etched starkly in the sky. I got a vision of the Buena Vista Crest and Merced Peak, shimmering in the distance. Knowing that it had not snowed in two weeks, I deemed the conditions auspicious.

I set off the next morning at 7 a.m. from Badger Pass with Fischer RCS skating skis and a fanny pack. Next stop, Mammoth Mountain. I took some PowerBars, a bivvy sack and Ensolite pad, but no backpack, stove or sleeping bag. I felt I had what I needed to survive. Even if I got hurt, I could have lasted for a while back there. I had called each of my strong skiing pals, Tim Messick on the west side and John Moynier on the east, who would know where to look if I did not return.

Over the long day, I found the deeper connection to the terrain and conditions I was seeking. Slopes that I would cruise down asleep

High peaks of Yosemite's backcountry   Photo: Cliff DeYoung

on heavy metal boards, I had to ski with total awareness of the finer scale of slope, crust and corn, cool blue powder, and wind-scoured ice. But one wrong turn, and I would have broken my little carbon toothpicks, and suffered a very long trudge back.

I spent the long February night traversing the north face of Triple Divide Peak. Twice in the night I stopped and napped in my bivvy sack, until I started shivering. Then I got back up to keep on sliding. One time I got into overly steep terrain and started kicking steps down in the dark, until I came to a cliff edge, the bottom of which was too far away for the headlamp beam to reach. I headed back up and found another way.

Dawn was spectacular on the top of Long Mountain. It took an hour for the sun to soften the steep slope I had to descend. I kicked with my little boots down through the cornices, using the skis as alpenstocks, then swooped big turns with echoing yells. No one was around to hear but me and the Clark's Nutcrackers, large birds that, amazingly, winter up there.

Later I was back on frozen crust traversing a vortex circling down to a frozen lake. It did not look possible on my edgeless skis until I noticed the pattern of texture of the snow, which had melted and refrozen in little lines all heading one direction. I found it enough to keep my skis going straight if I stayed in the correct orientation. The rest of the morning was miles of contour, where the skating skis really shined for high-speed traversing across the headwaters of the San Joaquin.

The crux descent was the final slope down to Twin Island Lakes. Entering the slope, I traversed across some nice wind board, saying to myself "Don't stop, you'll just get scared." Then I looked back and saw my tiny tracks like dull knife marks in the slope, and the 300-foot cliff below my line.

Late that evening after a big climb up to Catherine Lake and an awesome descent to Thousand Island Lake on blown-in powder, I took a wrong turn and headed all the way down to the San Joaquin River instead of up to Deadman Pass. By this time I was beyond bonked, headlamp batteries gone, and lost in the volcanic zone around Devils Postpile. The grain of the granite landscape that I had been so easily following devolved into complete volcanic chaos. Creeks seemed to be flowing the wrong way. I kept thinking that I would top out on the plateau of Agnew Meadow, only to hit another ridge top and struggle down the other side. Stumbling and frustrated, I just started heading east thinking I would hit the desert by morning. At last I skied onto the road down by Reds Meadow. After a long skate back to Minaret Pass, I was heading down the road into town.

I was so psyched! After 36 hours and nothing but PowerBars to eat, I was starving to death. A steak dinner at the Mammoth Mountain Inn was two downhill miles ahead! All of a sudden, the tracks I was following veered left, I was bombing down a hill, and it took five minutes to realize I followed rental snow machine tracks to an Inyo Crater overlook, the wrong road. It's ironic because I set out on this trip to make a statement about lack of technology, and then when I finally encountered groomed snow, it completely screwed me up. The end games on these things are always hard.

Back up the hill, at last I hit the lodge half an hour after the kitchen closed. I took the last shuttle into town, and the only place open was a dive pizza-and-wings joint. All I had was an Amex card which the dude wouldn't take. I offered to leave my gear and come back and pay in the morning but he wasn't having it. Finally, desperate I said, "Feed me or call an ambulance!" He pulled some quarters out of the tip jar and gave me a slice, just enough to hobble to Motel 6 where a young woman worker gave me quarters off my Amex card. I devoured all the crackers in the vending machine and fell asleep.

I was really happy with the results of the effort, though I also learned and modified my approach for future journeys, most notably with better food. Energy bars are useless after about four hours. On all future trips I took salmon meat, cheese, dried fruit – real food – and didn't get so crazed by the end.

It was a rash solo, but it wasn't stupid. John and Tim, backcountry skiers who knew that route backwards and forwards, had my back. I appreciated how it unfolded. It was a big trip to do with 12 hours of inspiration and planning, but sometimes great solos happen that way.

George Durkee:
"Sin and Redemption"

Since the Civilian Conservation Corps built the Ostrander Ski Hut in 1940, thousands have enjoyed the warmth and shelter the cabin provides in Yosemite's snowy wilderness. More than a few of them underestimated the arduous ten-mile trek to reach the refuge beside Ostrander Lake at 8,500 feet. Laborious trail breaking, the aptly named Heart Attack Hill and route finding in dark and stormy conditions thwart even experienced cross country skiers.

A National Park Service ranger since 1971 who helped oversee Ostrander for 20 years, George Durkee stood a far greater chance of helping those lost in Yosemite than getting lost there himself. A skier with decades of backcountry experience, Durkee accomplished both feats simultaneously in February of 1996 when he was 44.

I always liked living in winter terrain and enjoyed staying at Ostrander and skiing every day. That's the best and only way to get good at it. And people you meet there are almost always really nice, intelligent and enthusiastic. Though in the early years, we probably went out three or four times a week to help folks who didn't show up by 9 or 10 p.m. Quite often we'd find them huddled under a tree, on Heart Attack Hill or off route in the Illilouette drainage. They would always be happy to see us, especially the ones cold, shivering and wet without bivvy gear in wind that was blowing snow sideways.

This may not look good on my résumé, but in the really, really big winter of '95 and '96, I got lost in severe weather skiing to the hut.

Ostrander Hut   Photo: Dan Johanson

This even though I was a park ranger and assistant hutmeister, skiing over terrain I'd covered several hundred times! A review of my mistakes and correct decisions may help others.

A severe storm had been predicted, but hey, I'm the ranger! The weather was still okay when I left Badger Pass at my usual "crack of noon" start, overcast and snowing lightly with little wind. I was cheerfully following the tracks of a party of skiers ahead of me. Snowfall was increasing, but there was still no serious wind in the forest. At dusk around 5 p.m., I reached the base of Heart Attack Hill only a mile and a half from the hut.

The weather immediately went to heck. The trail at this point emerges from a fairly dense lodgepole forest onto an open slope. Winds gusted at about 30 miles per hour with blowing snow reducing visibility to about 50 feet. No problem, I'm the ranger and only 30 minutes from home. Heh, heh, heh, heh.

So I kept trudging along, head down, an old skier in a snow storm dreaming of hot tea. In the dark I could still make out the trail of the party ahead of me, but the storm was rapidly filling the tracks in. No need for a headlamp, though! Did I mention I'm the ranger?

Coming around the last hill and only about three quarters of a mile from the hut, I bumped into a bunch of lost and semi-frozen campers. "The ranger's here, we're saved, huzzah!" They'd lost the trail and I was faithfully following their tracks. Oops.

Okay, no problem. Time to take out my headlamp and find the trail, marked by yellow metal signs on the trees, spaced 30 to 50 feet apart. Fortunately most of them have reflective tape which shows up really well when a light hits them. As we're milling around, another group joins us, following these same errant tracks. There are now 12 people with only two headlamps amongst us. Winds blowing at 40 miles per hour, visibility dropping to 15 feet, pitch black. National parks are winter wonderlands!

It took a couple of minutes, though I did find the trail which was only 50 feet away, or so I thought. It took 30 minutes for everyone to adjust gear before we started off. The time it takes to do anything with a group increases exponentially with the size of the group. But within minutes, I realized I'd led everyone further off the trail and onto some unrecognizable ridge. I hate it when that happens. I hadn't seen a marker for awhile, but I was sure that if we just continued up the gully we were in, it would cross the trail only a hundred yards up the hill. And it would have if only we'd been going the right direction, which we weren't.

Now I come to full attention. We'd been so close to the hut when I found everyone, I really wasn't taking the situation all that seriously, figuring we'd just stumble in a little late. Now, though, I was authentically lost and sure didn't want to compound my embarrassment by getting even more screwed up. Time to reevaluate and buckle down.

Stop, regroup, and follow our tracks back to the last visible sign. It took about 20 minutes, but we found where I'd missed the trail. A few were suggesting that it might be time to bivvy. Not a bad idea, but I really, really knew where we were and I knew we could make it in now that I had my act together. At this point, I gave a pep talk. Put the person with the other headlamp at the end of the line and anchored on the marker that was visible. Then we stretched out the line until the next marker was visible and moved slowly along like some giant inch worm, always anchored on the last trail marker.

It wasn't getting any warmer out there. Most people were pretty well dressed for the conditions, but a couple weren't and if we didn't get in soon, we would have to bivvy. A few are authentically worried but I know we're on track now. After maybe 30 minutes, I can smell the smoke from the hut's woodstove. A few more trudging steps and, 20 feet away, the hut appears out of the gloom. We're saved from my stupidity! An hour and a half to go three quarters of a mile. Whew!

Lessons from this tale of sin and redemption? Number one is beware of hubris. Pay attention to what's going on and don't be overconfident. At the first sign you're lost, go back to your last known point. In any search and rescue operation I've been involved in – including almost my own! – people always make several bad decisions, so to recognize early that things are going badly and correct your mistakes is key. Don't plunge on ahead because the trail is "just over that hill." It isn't. Never has been, never will be.

Lesson number two: take the right gear. Carry a good headlamp. Most of the group was reasonably equipped to bivvy, but a couple were not. One guy dressed in something like racing gear and depended on his efforts to keep warm. When we stopped and herded up as we tried to figure out where we were, he got really cold and shivered. A woman was extremely cold and starting to lose it. They could have taken the time to dig into their packs and unbury their coats and they probably should have. That's lesson number three: get warm before you get cold. Keep the gear handy and put it on before you need it.

The folks at the hut had a big fire going, and everyone was mighty glad to get there, myself included.

Chandlee Harrell: "Surprises"

Going up is optional. Coming down is mandatory. Though many climbers know this basic mountaineering axiom, descents continue to see a large percentage of their complications.

Chandlee Harrell didn't seem to have a problem going up. His speed records on El Capitan's West Buttress and Salathé Wall testify to that. Once he climbed Astroman and The Rostrum, both demanding 5.11c routes, on a single day. Harrell regarded Snake Dike, a popular 5.7 line up the southwest face of Half Dome, as a pleasant afternoon diversion which he could comfortably climb unroped. However, coming down from the snowy summit proved more problematic to the 36-year-old in February of 1996.

I like to get in a good workout when I'm in the mountains. I'd been visiting a friend in Yosemite Valley and hadn't gotten much climbing done yet. Though it was February, it had been sunny for a while. From what I could see, the top of Half Dome was nice and clear. Getting to the top and back is a great aerobic workout. I knew the approach would be snowy but I decided I needed a little adventure before driving home and this was it.

My plan was to hike up to Snake Dike, free solo the climb, go over the top of the dome and down the cables[1] on the other side. I took only my shoes, chalk bag, a long sling to clip into the bolts if I needed, my headlamp, a windbreaker, a few PowerBars and water. I

1. Half Dome's cables remain on the hikers' route all year, though park staff removes their posts in winter months. As a result, they lay directly on the rock where snow covers them until the spring thaw.

started the approach around 2 p.m. and didn't expect a lot of trouble.

It was a beautiful day, one of those cool, crisp, sunny winter days with clear skies. The trail was pretty clear of snow up until Vernal Falls. By the top of Nevada Falls, thick and icy snow covered the trail the whole way. In the middle of winter there's nobody around there, which of course is part of the draw.

Before Little Yosemite Valley, I turned off towards Snake Dike. At that point you leave the trail and the footprints disappear. I had to posthole knee-deep through snow most of the way, which is kind of exhausting. I was counting on a workout but I didn't know how hard a workout I would get!

It's always tricky getting there but I'd been up to Snake Dike before and knew what the base looks like. I started climbing in the late afternoon with the sun hitting the rock. The route ascends a beautiful slab of low-angle granite which goes on forever. The position is spectacular, looking over Glacier Point and Yosemite Valley. There's one 5.7 friction move near the bottom. Then the rest of the climb is quite easy as it snakes its way up the side of Half Dome. In some places the granite knobs are as big as your hand. I'm not a big solo climber though I've run out a few climbs in my day. I like this kind of climbing because it's fun and not really scary. But there's no room for failure when you climb without a rope.

The pitches went by and I reached the top ledge where the route obviously stops. From there you're just a third of the way up. You still have to walk quite a distance and find your way to the top. Thankfully I have a fairly good sense of direction, which became relevant later.

I got up to the summit and the view was stunning. The sun had set and pink and purple colors filled the sky all over the high country. In pure peace I ate my PowerBars. Then I started to get chilly and I remembered that time was not on my side.

I walked over to where I thought the cables were and saw nothing but snow. The cables were buried. I couldn't see them and the slope was too steep to descend without them. It dawned on me there was no way I was getting down through there. The realization hit me with a massive jolt. There I was with no bivvy sack and only a light jacket to protect me from the elements. It was about to get very cold

Snake Dike on a snowy Half Dome

on this midwinter night near 9,000 feet.

My mind races at a time like this. What are the options, what should I do? Find a bivvy cave, dig a hole, spend the night? I thought about sleeping up there. But if I made it through the night, I'd still have the same problem the next day. There weren't a lot of choices. On full adrenaline I ran back to the other side towards Snake Dike. I thought I had a reasonable chance of climbing down it. The crux would be finding the top of the route, in the waning light, amidst the vast expanse of the southwest flank of Half Dome. Otherwise, I wasn't sure I'd survive the night. I wasn't about to chance it. My heart was pounding. It was getting dark quickly and I didn't have much time.

Luckily I recognized some of the landmarks I'd passed when I hiked up. Cut down this corner system, duck behind that boulder, head down this slab, drop off that lip. I had only one chance to get it right before it was too dark to make out the terrain. I found the top of the climb just as it got really dark. It was a critical milestone, and I allowed myself a short moment to rejoice. But I still had to down climb the route this night.

I donned my headlamp, switched back into my climbing shoes and started down the climb. It was a pitch dark night, and I climbed down, focused in my little bubble of light and tense perspiration, pitch after pitch. Every so often I'd stop and look at the lights in the valley. I also saw some skiers' headlamps moving around at Glacier Point. If they saw my headlamp, they must have wondered why a single light was going down Half Dome in the dark.

That 5.7 move made me a little more nervous in the middle of the night. I had never expected to see it again that day but the move passed and I made it down to terra firma. Climbing up had been a lot more fun. Relief rushed through me. I knew I could make it out from there. I just had to walk back through my own postholes. After I changed my shoes I found my tracks and followed them. I thought the adventure was over.

But Mother Nature decided to throw another curve ball at me. Pretty soon I saw another pair of footprints right next to my own. These were mountain lion tracks following mine. I was hit with another jolt! And my wave of happiness quickly disappeared. My neck bristled and I started scanning the trees and terrain around me. Why was a mountain lion following my tracks? Was I on his agenda? I was afraid he'd jump on my back at any minute. So I picked up a large stick and tried to look as big as I could. I shouted as I postholed my way back through the forest. He followed my tracks all the way out to the main trail. I was on a razor's edge the whole way but he didn't bother me.

I reached the valley by 11 p.m. This was a Sunday and I had to work the next day, so there was nothing for it but to drive home to the Bay Area. You've got to be careful driving late at night after these adventures that we do. Sometimes that's the most hair-raising part of the outing.

My big error was assuming what Half Dome is like in February. I assumed the snow had melted off on the north side but it doesn't at that time of year. It would have been a much different story if I hadn't found the top of the climb.

If you climb in the middle of winter, you're going to get a little bit of adventure. I like to push the edge and see what's out there and what surprises nature has in store, though this kind of stuff isn't for everyone. I'd say do it only if you really enjoy the backcountry and going out in it. Always be prepared and try to think through all outcomes. Consider every precaution you can take, like carrying bivvy gear in case something like this happens. And make sure you know your descent route!

I also recommend ingraining the habit of paying attention to your surroundings and keeping track of landmarks on your way. That was critical in my situation. A final note is to always let people know where you're going so they can find you more quickly in the event something happens. I didn't do that in this case. My situation didn't bode well when I first recognized what was going on. It got a little bit crazy but I felt pretty good about extracting myself from trouble.

Majka Burhardt:
"Epic Desire"

Those drawn to the mountains enjoy their solitude, but in a mecca like Yosemite, crowds can form even on towering granite walls. Consequently, climbers learn through experience both outdoors etiquette and how to respond to those who break it.

So it was with Majka Burhardt, then 19, in October of 1996. Visiting Yosemite for her first time, the future guide and author and her partner tackled Sentinel Rock's Chouinard-Herbert route (5.11c/A2), negotiating social difficulties along with the vertical terrain.

The first time I went to Yosemite, I tried to skip major parts of the Yosemite experience. I stayed at Lower Pines instead of Camp 4, I avoided El Cap and I never brought a headlamp on a climb because I never planned to use one. I was 19 and I had all of the experience of one summer of alpine rock climbing in the Cascades to steer my decisions. I thought this was plenty. Who wouldn't, with a ringer for a partner?

Eli was 11 years older than me and had spent all of that additional time climbing and guiding. I did what any hungry young climber does when she has a more seasoned partner: I co-opted Eli's experience and made it my own. We flew around the valley, granite line to granite line. And then we hit Sentinel Rock.

The Chouinard-Herbert route was our goal. We had friends spending the day on the nearby Steck-Salathé. The four of us had a leisurely breakfast and wandered up to the cliff at 8. Gardiner, Joe, and Eli's combined experience was at least 30 times greater than mine, an easy figure to calculate when you have only really been climbing for a year.

The approach seemed quick and straightforward. We passed two French guys going the wrong way and felt automatically better about our collective precision. I was second in line in our group of four. If pressed, I would have admitted then to my relative position of inexperience in the group, but if not pressed, I would have pretended otherwise. Right behind the person who knew where he was going seemed a great place to draw that pretend line.

At 15 pitches, Chouinard-Herbert would likely take us the good part of the day. It never occurred to me that it might take more. Never mind that I'd never climbed a route more than 1,500 feet tall before. Eli and I wished Gardiner and Joe a good climb on Steck-Salathé and settled into swapping pitches on our route's opening, low-angled pitches. I was belaying at the top of the Chessman Pinnacle when I heard the first "Allo?"

The next glimpse I had of the Frenchman was his hand pulling on my anchor. His foot skimmed my hip and he straddled my belay stance and started reaching through. Right about then, Eli yelled "off belay" from above. I tried not to look up and into the Frenchman's aqua cotton tights while I confirmed Eli's call.

The Frenchman completed his move and stood beside me. I craned my neck and saw Eli just as he saw the Frenchman. What happened next was not my fault.

"Mmmmmhhhmm...Frenchies...mm," Eli yelled.

"Frenchies?" the Frenchman asked. His hand was still on my anchor.

"Non," I said. And then, "Oui?" I tried again. "Commont s'appelle..." That wasn't right either. How do you say in French, I wondered, that your climbing partner is not a fan of French climbers? That he'd been stymied time and again around the world by this man's countrymen? That "the Frenchies" were out to get us and keep us from our maximum climbing goals?

At least I had to prove to him that I knew some French so I said, "Je gargarize." The man raised his eyebrows. I don't know why I decided that conjugating the French word for gargle that my high school teacher made us use to perfect our r's seemed like a good idea

Chouinard-Herbert on Sentinel Dome   Photo: Dan Johanson

three pitches up on Sentinel. But it distracted the Frenchman long enough for me to scurry past him onto the slab above.

I made the moves as quickly as I could but each time my foot left a hold, the Frenchman's hand appeared on that hold. Rudely he climbed right up behind me. I was annoyed but wanted to handle it delicately. The 5.9 went quickly. The 5.10c slowed me down. I picked up a foot, put it back down and stepped on the Frenchman's hand.

"Yow!" he yelled.

I stalled. "Ok?" I asked.

"I go?" he asked.

I thought about it. He was fast in his aqua tights, faster than me. The rope pulled on me, hard. Eli knew how to haul, and at that point, I knew he would not be afraid to do so. "French…reeeeee," he called.

I grimaced. "My climbing partner is a bigot," I thought, "and I will have to pay the price." I craned my head as far back on the wall as I could so I could see Eli. I frowned, hoping he could sense my displeasure from 60 feet away.

"French free!" he yelled again. He made large pantomiming motions of grabbing the anchor and pulling himself toward it. "Now!"

I saw the Frenchman's face harden.

"He doesn't mean that," I said to him in English. "Stop saying that!" I yelled to Eli. The rope only pulled harder.

I grabbed the carabineers, swung my body up and pulled on gear again. Each move made me angrier. I could climb 5.10c, maybe not as fast as my partner wanted but I could do it. I knew Eli well enough to know that letting the Frenchman arrive at the belay before me would scar our climbing relationship. Then I would become part of his French curse. I kept going.

When I reached the anchor, Eli grabbed at the gear on my harness. "You might have to French free again," he said.

I huffed, shook my head and swatted his hands away from my harness. "You're a bigot," I said.

Eli looked at my quizzically.

"French free?" I said. "Seriously, Eli. That's cruel."

Eli started to smile. "Do you even know what it means?"

"Other than that you're an awful American?"

"Majka," he said, "give me some credit. It just means pulling on gear." He gestured to the stack of gear dangling from the rope near my tie-in point. "Something you clearly at least know how to do."

"Oh," I said. "I'm…" I was sorry, I just couldn't seem to say it. I was, after all, the one who had to deal with the man in tights. It seemed better to be in Eli's position, at the head of the conga line, than at the bottom working on your diplomacy.

We continued up the route, Eli leading the next hard pitch while I waited for the Frenchmen. I could hear their calls but I never saw another flash of aqua. Eli and I went back to swinging leads as the climbing got easier, and then back to his leading as it got harder. I had told him I'd wanted and expected to lead equal pitches but my obstinacy faded the further we got from the Frenchmen. Eventually I just followed.

I spent my time at the belays fantasizing about the Frenchies. They were probably staying at Camp 4. I still hadn't technically been inside of Camp 4, even though I'd been in Yosemite for two weeks. I told other climbers that it was just better at Lower Pines, even though I didn't know what it was better than. The Frenchies probably ate canned food they pillaged from a dumpster; I had four packages of almond cheese in our cooler. Granted, I was road tripping for two months in a 1983 Saab. But they were probably hitchhiking.

We made good time. The Afro-Cuban Flakes came into view and Eli wound his way underneath them with finesse. I followed, and without him even asking me to, I French freed. We summited three pitches later. We waited at the top for Gardiner and Joe, and started down all together. The complicated and exposed descent was easy if you didn't have to be the one making the decisions. Eli told the other guys about the Frenchmen and my French freeing. We all laughed.

"They are probably having an epic up there," someone said.

And then I knew. I wanted the epic. I wanted to relish in my mistakes and turn them into grand stories after I stumbled down from eventual success.

Instead, we slid onto the Four-Mile Trail just as the night went black. While the Frenchies got benighted on Sentinel, soon we had beers in our hands. The taste of the cold alcohol, my comfortable Therm-a-Rest and the following day's rest quickly cured me of my epic desire. Who would really want an epic, anyway?

Noah Kaufman:
"Miracle"

Climbers in distress from fatigue, weather or the difficulty of the task at hand rightfully trust their properly-used gear to protect against catastrophe. Many will lose sleep to learn that a single mistake can cause the most terrifying equipment failure imaginable. Such was the shocking near-death experience of three men climbing high on El Capitan in June of 1999.

Noah Kaufman, 24, was visiting the park for the first time. Then a medical student from Tulane University in New Orleans, he later became a doctor of emergency medicine at Yosemite Medical Clinic. Kaufman, his friend Bernard Guest and their new acquaintance who became known as "Falling Noah" started up The Nose (5.13b/A2) in search of a 34-pitch adventure. Few have returned from any climb with a more unforgettable and life-changing experience.

When I first arrived in the valley, my jaw dropped to my knees. I didn't know anything like that could exist in the world. It was way more impressive than anything I had seen up to that point in my life. I was absolutely pinching myself trying to take it all in and not believing what I was seeing. Every minute I had to stop, get out of the car and look around. I couldn't stop smiling. It seemed like the best place ever.

After my first year of medical school, I was psyched to get out and climb. A couple of friends and I came to Yosemite for a month, mostly to climb boulders like Midnight Lightning. I was so excited to be free that I dyed my hair green before I showed up in the valley. I knew the big wall of medical school and residency I had in front of me.

Up until then I had never really even considered climbing big cliffs, but suddenly it was obvious why those things had to be climbed, and I felt I would probably end up on one of them. One of my good friends who came along was Bernard Guest, who was more into technical aid climbing than I and he was really psyched to do a big wall.

"Do you want to do The Nose?" he asked.

"Which one's The Nose?" I said. I really didn't know much about aid climbing and had never done a big wall. We went to El Cap Meadow and he pointed it out. I thought it looked incredible and we decided to do it.

Because we'd never been on it and since I had done zero aid climbing before, we went to the Camp 4 bulletin board looking for another partner. We found a guy named Noah with long blond hair who looked like a rocker and we hit it off. He told us he was a 5.13 climber and had done The Nose before. "Perfect!" we thought. "This guy's going to take us up and show us the ropes." But it didn't turn out that way.

We all contributed gear, racked everything and loaded our pig[1]. The Nose starts with mostly slabby climbing. I led the first pitch. On the first day we climbed four pitches to Sickle Ledge. Noah rapped to the ground to sleep that night. Bernard and I wanted to really experience the wall, so we slept on the ledge. Noah came back in the morning and we had a really fun day climbing the Stoveleg Cracks. We were leapfrogging and taking turns leading. I learned how to jumar and the three of us were getting our system down. But we only made it to Dolt Tower on the second day when we had intended to get to El Cap Tower.

At the end of day two we started to realize that maybe we didn't have enough food and water. We thought the climb would take three days but we weren't moving as fast as we thought we would. I was pretty much the strongest free climber of us and I led as much as I could. I did some aid climbing and some French free now and then. Bernard was a methodical superstar. We thought Noah would be a lot stronger, but he was falling on things a lot easier than 5.13. Maybe

---

1. pig: climbers' slang for a haul bag

The Nose on El Capitan

he had done The Nose before, but it just didn't seem like it. The rock doesn't lie, and he really didn't seem to know what he was doing. But neither did we and he was a nice enough guy so Bernard and I decided to roll with it.

Eagle Ledge is a decent-sized ledge but not huge, about a foot wide and five feet long. The three of us barely fit on it. At this point, you're 18 pitches up and the climb becomes more vertical. Noah took the lead while I belayed him and Bernard hauled up the pig. Noah was jamming and lying back and he clips into a cam about seven feet up from the ledge. Then he climbs higher to about 15 feet above the ledge. He'd made some remarks earlier on the climb that seemed to show he was scared, and he looked insecure liebacking this pitch.

"Oh man, guys, I think I'm going to fall," he said.

That was kind of a weird thing to say and Bernard and I looked at each other, confused. This guy told us he climbed 5.13, and now he seemed real scared and intimidated climbing 5.9.

Finally I said, "Okay, fall. You're on belay, man. You'll be okay." So he did. What happened next took place in an instant but I could replay it in my mind for eternity.

He fell and he didn't just slip off the rock. He jumped outward from it. Maybe he didn't want to hit the ledge and break an ankle. But when he jumped out, he made the rope tight going from me into the one piece he placed, into a crack and around a sharp corner to his harness. Bernard and I were watching and all of a sudden there was an explosion. A cloud of sparkling dust filled the air and Noah fell straight down. He landed on the ledge and came to a complete stop. I can remember a lot of things in my life but nothing with more vivid clarity than that moment.

At first we thought that this fixed piece had blown out of the crack, but that wasn't it. Noah had two feet of rope hanging from his harness. I was the first person who realized what had happened. The brand new rope serrated instantly on a sharp arête during his fall. Most climbers use a runner in that spot to protect the rope but Noah hadn't done that. He had landed on the small ledge through sheer luck. He stood there unprotected and didn't even know it. I grabbed his daisy chain and clipped him into the anchor with a carabiner without even stopping to think.

"Guys, the piece did not blow," I told them. Then they both saw the rope's cut ends, one on Noah's harness and one on my belay. We had this long moment of silence while we all visualized him falling a thousand feet and becoming a ketchup smear on the slabs below. Noah's shirt was off and I could see his heart pounding as he put it together. Then he knelt at the belay and started sobbing.

"Guys, I'm out of here! I'm done. Let's bail, let's bail now!" Noah cried. He was obviously horrified. I really felt for him but I was undecided about whether to keep going or not. But Bernard said, "Hell no, we're going to the top." He grabbed the serrated end of the belay rope, tied a figure eight knot into his harness, grabbed the rack and jumped onto the pitch. So we just kept going.

During the next three days we ran out of food and water so we started drinking whatever nasty stuff we could find. Most parties bring too much water and leave it behind, so The Nose has old milk jugs and half-full Gatorade bottles behind cracks and on ledges all over it. They had been sitting there so long that the water tasted like liquid plastic.

Other things went wrong. We dropped some aid gear and an ascender so someone had to use a prusik knot the rest of the way. Then the pig got stuck before the Great Roof and in several little chimneys. We had to rappel down and free it. And the whole way up, we were all scared to death that the rope would cut again. I was convinced that I would die before the top of the climb. Noah had almost died and at a certain point I got so tired that I became resigned to it. We were so inexperienced and in so far over our heads.

But we also saw some amazing things on the way. The climbing was immaculate and world-class. One day these huge raindrops fell. There was an updraft of wind up The Nose, and for a moment it froze all these globular, vibrating raindrops in midair. It was a really weird phenomena and one of the coolest things I've ever seen.

After Noah dodged his incredible bullet, we made a compromise so that he would continue up the route willingly: he would not have to lead any more pitches and we would belay him even when he was jugging[2] or hauling the pig. He was strictly along for the ride from that point on. Noah was pretty quiet the rest of the way. Somehow

---

2. jugging: climbing a rope with ascenders

we made it, which is 100 percent thanks to Bernard. I learned a lot from watching Bernard stand up the way he did and say, "This is just one thing that happened, and it could have been a lot worse."

We were psyched when we got up there. We took pictures and gave high-fives. It was definitely a bonding experience. But we weren't done yet. A rattlesnake came along hissing at us and we couldn't get around it. After all we'd been through, we couldn't believe it. We threw rocks and finally got it to slither off. Then we had no idea how to get back down. Noah started taking us west, which is the wrong way. We hauled all our gear and followed him a while before we saw some other climbers trucking past us the other way. So we followed them to the East Ledges descent and finally got down that way.

All I could think about was Cheetos and a steak. We went straight to eat and spent all the little money we had on a carpe diem, mega dinner. I bought a Dr. Pepper and a chocolate milk. This experience was an exciting story to tell in the dining room though there were some climbers who never believed it. People began calling me "Catching Noah" and him "Falling Noah."

I've never seen a rope cut like that and I think it was a miracle if ever I saw one. It was pretty unbelievable the way he landed on the small ledge and that he didn't tumble off it or even hurt himself in the fall. If it happened 100 more times, I really don't think it would turn out that way again. I'm not a religious person, but it made me think that maybe he had a guardian angel. Maybe it wasn't his time. I don't know what, but there was something going on. I maintain my agnosticism about the whole thing.

That first big wall was the ultimate trial by fire for me, and I thought I'd never do another one, ever. The Nose was the most crazy, horrible, amazing, and way-too-intense experience I'd ever had. But of course I went back and I've done a bunch of big walls since. Now that I know what I'm doing, they're a lot more fun.

The biggest lesson from it all was that I have to be totally competent and rely on myself in any kind of situation that involves life or death. Even if I'm with someone who is more experienced than me, I have to personally make sure that I know what the hell is going on, instead of trusting someone I don't know to take me up The

Nose, for instance. That experience gave me more self-reliance and confidence. Now I trust myself the most, because at least I know that I can be honest with myself, and if I get in over my head, then I can reach out to get help. I know I shouldn't try to do something that I'm not prepared to do. That's translated to my experience in medicine. I wanted to get through my residency without hurting or killing someone, and sometimes that meant admitting I didn't know something that I should have known. So it also checked my ego and humbled me. The Nose puts you in your place no matter who you are.

I cut off about ten feet of the rope and tied it around my steering wheel. Several cars later, I still have it, and you can see the side that I cut neatly and the other side that exploded. I'm sure Noah has his end of the rope, too, though we parted ways and I never saw or heard from him again. Sometimes I look at the rope and think of him, that lucky bastard.

Jim Zellers:
"The Half-a-Brain Project"

Walking down the north face of Half Dome using its raised steel cables intimidates many hikers. Snowboarding down the steep, avalanche-prone slope was unthinkable until Jim Zellers, 35, applied five years of study and sweat to the project which concluded in March of 2000.

A world-class snowboarder with first descents on New Zealand's Mt. Cook (12,316 feet), Alaska's Mt. Denali (20,320 feet) and Nepal's Pumori (23,494 feet), Zellers also became an accomplished rock climber and skier prone to crisscrossing Yosemite's backcountry in winter. His friend and fellow mountaineer Richard Leversee partnered with him on an effort that proved the value of patience and persistence.

Whenever I see Half Dome, it always blows me away. After thousands of times, I still can't enter Yosemite Valley without really being taken aback. It's a powerful place and Half Dome resides over the top of everything. Half Dome seems to just draw you in from every angle. I've climbed on it and hiked on the cables. And of course, what a crazy piece of stone it is geomorphically.

Snowboarding feels natural to me, with one foot pointed forward and one foot trailing, like when you run and slide on a kitchen floor. It's my favorite thing that I'd go do every day if I could. To combine the two became an intriguing project. I thought this had to happen.

So I measured the route in the summer and I found the steepness to be within reason. The steepest part I found was 47 degrees, not as steep as I thought it would be. My first time checking the route out in winter came when a friend of mine was getting his pilot's license. He had to do a mountain flight, he asked if I wanted to go and I said, "Sure." So he and his instructor flew me over the dome and I saw there wasn't enough snow.

Every year after that I'd wait for the right snow conditions. I knew I had to go slowly and really absorb what was happening out there. Snow science was a big part of the project, learning how snow sticks to rock. It became a project that Richard and I did together. Richard always called it "The Half-a-Brain Project." He figured it took half a brain to do it, though he didn't know which half.

What was the weather forecast? What were the temperatures? What were the wind directions? And what were the temperature changes forecast to be throughout the storm? That was the biggest factor. If we got the right temperature changes throughout the storm, then we knew we'd probably get the right snow conditions. When was the last storm? What was the wind direction? There were all these things we had to add up. The science was as much fun as anything else.

In that first year, I hiked out to see it and climbed maybe 100 feet up the dome. There wasn't enough snow but I could still start to get the feel of it. We never got the right storm cycle that year. There was often an east wind after a storm, and an east wind would strip the stone. But we knew if the wind stayed west, and if it would be cloudy after a storm, that would give us a day to set up and get out there. We really never got a chance again until the next year in December. We got up there, and again, it wasn't happening.

One hard thing is, you can't even see the north face from the valley or anywhere without hiking out to it. When I was trying to get information, I called the Tuolumne winter rangers, who ski every day and monitor the snow pack.

"How's the stability on the domes?" I ask.

"Stay away from the domes," he says.

I tried again but I couldn't get him to say anything except "stay away from the domes." So I hung up and I was back to square one.

Hiking the Mist Trail isn't bad in the winter. If you're moving well, it takes about three hours to get to the cables. I'd always get on that trail and people would see the snowboard sticking out of my pack. It was so hard to get through a whole line of people asking questions. "Are you going snowboarding up there?" We couldn't stop with every person and explain it, so we came up with things to say like, "It's not a snowboard, it's a picnic table."

We never told people we were going to do it, because I think when you socially commit, you really blind your instincts. I knew if I left the entire world out of my decision-making process, I could just approach it with a really clear head. Richard and my wife Bonnie knew, but they were non-judgmental. I didn't want to have to come home every time and have people say, "Did you do it?" I didn't need the outside influence, which is really distracting.

One year Richard couldn't go. That was the year Bonnie went up with me instead. She was six months pregnant with our first kid at the time and showing pretty good. We got up there and there was almost six feet of snow on the dome, and I say, "This is perfect!" But there was a big crack in it. "Oh man, that's a bummer." There was one part where the snow almost connected, but for the most part, the crack was three feet wide.

"If you do this, I'm divorcing you!" my wife says.

"I'm just looking!" I say.

While I'm taking a picture of the dome for future reference, this whole left side of the snow slab falls off, boom! So it's a good thing I wasn't there.

Up and down the trail, up and down, every year for five years. If the trail was closed, we'd go anyway with crampons and a rope. It's sketchy in there though we never had to belay each other. But we really needed crampons and axes on the dome itself.

Finally one March we got there and I could see the snow was a little thin, but it covered the slope and looked all right.

"What do you think?" Richard says.

"I think I'm doing it," I say.

We had this sentimental goodbye moment and we parted ways. I assumed the snow was going to stick. By then I knew what sticky snow on domes looks like. But there were a lot of things I didn't know that I found out when I got up there. Richard stayed behind to take the pictures.

I started hiking up with my crampons and axe. I got to a point where the rock was a little bare. So I went up a tongue of snow off to the right of the cables that overhangs the valley. My front points were hitting the dome, so I hiked back and grabbed the cables. The cables weren't posted up but they were laying on the dome. I got higher to places with drum snow, six inches deep and two feet off the dome. If you step on it, it sounds like a drum. I knew if I busted through this, it would be disaster. For years I really worked on this mental image of not having a catastrophic failure. I went through this whole thing in my imagination. "Oh, I can snowboard around that. I've got to make this right turn. I've got to be focused through this zone." I think the number one thing I had to overcome was the fear of the whole thing.

It's beautiful to be on Half Dome on a sunny day in winter. I hiked all the way to the top and walked around. There's a huge, deep snowfield up there. It was great to be on this plateau of snow in the sky alone.

Before the run I felt intimidated and nervous but as I started I became calm and serene. The route was not a straight line. I had to make the most challenging and precise turns of my life, but it felt like time slowed down and the movements were fresh and easy. As you start, all you see is Mt. Watkins. You can't see the route as you're going into the abyss. I started out right of the cables, then on top of them, then left quite a ways. I saw Mt. Starr King. In my mind I was flipping out, inspired and in awe. I got into a rhythm and went through the drum snow section. The exposure was absolutely phenomenal. I got close to the edge but I wasn't about to go over it. At the time I was so ready for it. It took about five minutes which flew by quickly.

Before I knew it I pulled out at the bottom thinking, "Wow, it's over." Both of us were euphoric, in shock.

"That was so rad!" I say.

"You should do it again," Richard says.

So I did and this time Richard hiked back up there with me too. But the snow had already started to melt. On one section where it really overhangs, I was making a heel turn and the snow broke and my nose went straight down. Now I'm pointing down the absolutely wrong fall line. I quickly corrected and came out okay. So that was the one time where I got a little too excited. I wanted to do it again but I should have let it go. It was a reality check and a reminder that I could make a mistake. Fortunately it didn't lead to a bad conclusion.

It stayed hot that day, T-shirt weather in the valley. We knew it was going to warm up and the next day the snow would be gone.

I learned that if you really want to do something, there's no need to include anyone else in it other than your immediate partners. Why do you need to tell the whole world until your project is finished?

I still use the technique of just imagining the actions before I do something difficult in snowboarding or climbing or biking. When I'm doing something really important, and there are consequences and I've got to stick it, I go through this process using every sense: visualization, sense of smell, sense of touch. I've got to hear the wind, smell the pine trees, feel the cold. I put myself in that zone and go through all those steps.

Another thing I constantly remember is that projects like this are really not that important. In the end, I'm not solving world hunger. I'm not fixing the health care system. I'm just one guy doing one thing. That holds true today. You see people who think that what they're doing is so great and so important that the entire world should rally behind them. I say, "You're not Mother Teresa here! You're just doing your little thing. Not that many people care, and you're not going to change anybody's life."

But don't get me wrong. We were psyched! I can't wait for someone else to do it. I would love to live through it again without me doing it because it's a great project. And if someone wants to do it, I could write out the recipe for the perfect storm cycle.

Ammon McNeely:
"Marooned on a Sea of Granite"

Yosemite's generally favorable climate contributes to its great popularity, though those who toil on scorching granite learn not to underestimate the park's fierce summer heat. Running out of water on a big wall like El Capitan's 18-pitch Eagle's Way (5.10a/A4) would rightfully terrify even the most bold and capable climbers.

Enter Ammon McNeely, who set an unprecedented 22 speed records on El Cap routes like The Reticent Wall, Plastic Surgery Disaster and Wall of Early Morning Light. The daredevil extraordinaire also counts slacklining, skydiving, BASE jumping and wingsuit flying among his pursuits. Yet McNeely would have never tempted fate again after August of 2000 had the 30-year-old not summoned his deepest reserves of physical and mental fortitude.

The early August sun beat on my back as I studied the route. I visualized myself ascending its cracks with great speed. I knew Yosemite Valley would see a scorching day. I looked at my watch and chuckled out loud. What a slacker, I thought. I had overslept by three hours. I convinced myself I needed the extra sleep for what I was about to attempt.

I showed up in the Valley having never climbed a big wall. In fact, I had only been climbing for two years and I wanted to solo El Capitan as my first wall. Determination and some advice from my friend Chongo helped me solo the North America Wall with only five pitons and a two-point hammock. Since then I'd practically made Yosemite my home, living on the wall as much as possible.

Even though I'd climbed this great monolith 14 times, four of them solo, I was taking a giant step toward the next level of climbing. My goal was to on-sight solo an El Capitan route in less than 24 hours. It was a very lofty goal and doubts lingered. I was pretty new to speed climbing and I'd never speed-soloed a wall. The route I chose was Eagle's Way, which nobody had ever soloed in a day. The attractive thing about the right side of El Cap is that all of the routes are really steep and overhanging, so you can take longer falls without hitting ledges. And it's El Cap, which is just a really good quality rock.

"What makes you think you can?" I asked myself. I tried to push the negative energy out. I can do this, I told myself. I felt I was ready. Then I looked up the cliff and got a bad case of butterflies. It didn't help the little argument that was going on inside my head.

Eagle's Way is a moderate aid line on the short side of the overhanging southeast face of El Cap. It goes through some of the darkest black diorite on the face. The temperature was rising and the black rock radiated heat beyond belief. I tried to stay focused while hydrating with extra water.

I racked my gear and gathered up the rations I intended to take. I put three gallons of water, four Clif Bars, a headlamp, a fleece jacket and hat into a small pack and started climbing. It was 9:45 a.m., a far cry from the 6 o'clock start I intended. I started off fast, maybe a little too fast. I free climbed 30 feet before I started aiding. I hooked past piton placements and back-cleaned gear[1] to save time. I came to a rivet a third of the way up the first pitch. I didn't think twice about it. I fetched a wired hanger off my rack, stepped up and placed a hook. I jumped on the hook, pinched my belay piece for slack and climbed my aid ladder.

I suddenly felt slack on the rope. I looked down just in time to watch, with horror, the wired hanger spiraling 50 feet down the rope! It smacked into a huge rock at the base, where I had tied the other end for an anchor. I was on only one hook, and that was all that separated me from crashing to certain death.

I was looking the Grim Reaper straight in the eyes. I took a few

---

1. back-cleaning: to remove gear beneath a climber before establishing a secure anchor, greatly increasing the risk of a catastrophic fall

Eagle's Way on El Capitan

deep breaths and calmly selected the biggest hook on my rack. I had to do a couple of hook moves and then I was able to get some protection in a crack. That felt a lot better and I relaxed. I continued without incident, arriving at the belay in less than 30 minutes.

The pitches fell quickly. I pulled out every trick in the book; loop belays, crazy-aid-man style and even free soloing. Soon I was covered in sweat. I had no chalk and my hands didn't want to stay in the cracks. Fatigue overcame me.

The sun was scorching. The temperature was over 100 and I felt light-headed and constantly thirsty. Drink, I kept reminding myself. Three gallons of water should be plenty. I was a third of the way up the route and I felt like I was cruising. I opened one bottle after another and dumped water down my throat, gasping and unable to catch my breath as it went down. I convinced myself there was no way of running out of water, so rationing wasn't even an issue.

I climbed pitch after pitch: leading, fixing the line, rappelling down to the low point, strapping on my pack and jumaring while cleaning to the high point. I felt like a human yo-yo. Not having to haul a big bag was great. It saved me lots of logistics that would have eaten time.

But the work involved was mind-numbing. I started to feel like I was floating in and out of some crazy dream. I was marooned on a sea of granite and I was sinking fast. I kept paddling, fighting to stay above water. Everything started to seem awfully scary. Bits and pieces of reality floated in. The Black Pillar. What was next? The Seagull. I felt like seagulls were picking at my brain, leaving me unable to think. What was happening?

I dug out the torn and tattered topo map to try to make sense of where I was. I just climbed the Seagull and I was at the tenth pitch. I looked at my watch: ten hours. Hey, not bad for a first speed solo. I smiled and congratulated myself.

As I groped in my pack for some much-deserved water, my smirk disappeared and my jaw dropped. No way! This isn't happening! I dug deeper. I frantically checked around the belay. I had no water, none! I accidentally left a gallon behind, and I was so caught up in the moment, I drank all I had without realizing it. I tried to breathe evenly as my pulse quickened and a thousand different things entered my mind.

"What now?" I asked myself. Do I continue? I thought about what most climbers would do in this situation. They would descend, without question. But I'm headstrong and not like most climbers. Also, I was about halfway up at a point where it would be really difficult to rappel. I had to choose to go up or down, and I chose up. Maybe it wasn't the smartest move, but it was bold.

As I started the next pitch, all at once everything seemed really dicey. I felt as though I could not make correct decisions. I was collapsing in my slings. I rappelled back to the belay and hung in my harness. I couldn't see myself giving up and descending to the ground. I also couldn't see myself getting rescued. I didn't want to die. The only thing left was to survive this ordeal and continue the climb.

I spent that whole night hanging in my harness. I became conscious sometime in the middle of the night. Half of my body had no feeling and was not responding. I lifted my dead arm with the other. It flopped back, paralyzed from being smashed against the wall. My leg couldn't move. My head was numb. I was afraid of being permanently paralyzed. I drifted out of consciousness.

In the morning I awoke, the sun splitting my head in two. My body still wasn't working. My leg loops on my harness had cut off circulation to my legs. I rubbed my arms and legs for 20 minutes until blood started finally flowing.

I thought about a water bottle, hanging from a belay, somewhere above me. I was so certain of this, because I saw it there while climbing Lost in America the previous week. The hope of water was a powerful motivator that kept me going.

Climbing was increasingly slow. At times, I couldn't even straighten my arms or legs. My entire body would cramp with dehydration and I just hung, curled in a fetal position, dry heaving profusely. Other times, I would find myself hanging from my daisy chain. Apparently I passed out while standing on my gear and had taken a dreaded fall.

Massive explosions were going off in my head. Then reality would find me again, stranded. I had nothing left to do but struggle upward, climbing more slowly than any other time in my life.

I continued and soon found myself in an A3, overhanging, squeeze chimney. Some beta floated into my head about this being the crux of the route. Awkward placements soon got me out of the squeeze-fest. Then the crack ran out and I couldn't negotiate the next correct sequence. I had to do something. I felt myself fading again and I didn't want to pass out and fall. I crimped an edge with my right hand, leaving my right foot in the aider. I smeared with my left foot and tried to place a small cam.

Pop! I shot down the granite like a missile, ripping three cams out of the rock like a zipper. I hung, passed out, after the 25-foot whipper. I came to with explosions going off in my reality. It felt like bombs were going off all around me. Fuzzy blotches appeared in my vision. I imagined my brain cells, popping like squashed grapes. I hung there dry heaving, wondering how I got into such a predicament. If only I could find that water bottle. I knew it was up there somewhere. My dry heaves subsided after 15 minutes or so.

It hurt to even think, but I continued. I soon found myself on a small ledge at the fourteenth pitch. It was around midnight and I'd only completed four pitches since daybreak. I was in full-on survival mode. I tried to urinate in my hand so that I could drink it. I would have drank a bottle of pee if I had one. I tried sucking on the rock. There was a very small amount of water running through a slot, and I thought maybe I could get some moisture out. Nothing happened. I was so dehydrated that my tongue swelled up to three times its normal size. I was choking on it. My throat felt like a swollen piece of leather. When I tried to swallow, I would gag. I kept praying the water bottle I'd seen would materialize.

I collapsed on the small ledge, half my body on and half off. I became unconscious for a few hours, time enough to dream about meeting my maker. I was almost relieved. Anything for this nightmare to be over.

I awoke with a new urgency. I climbed around the corner and got some amazing exposure. This lifted my spirits. New energy entered my body. I started up an amazing crack that gobbled cam hooks. The pitch was really beautiful but I couldn't enjoy it. I was a mess. The simplest thing like picking a half-inch cam off my rack was confusing and laborious. I would find myself out of breath constantly with a splitting headache. I gave up hope of coming across the water bottle that I had seen. Two more pitches to the top.

I continued to climb and soon came to a bolt ladder. I paused in a small alcove for shade at the belay. One more pitch. Beta again entered my head, something about avoiding the A2 to the summit. There should be some 5.9 variation instead, but I forced the thought of free climbing out of my mind. I was in no shape for such a struggle. I finished the A2 crack and crawled over the lip and toward a tree.

I made it. I looked at my watch, and 46 hours had gone by since I started this adventure. I half walked and half crawled to the top of Lost in America where I had hidden a cache of food and water the previous week. I was so confused that it took a while to find it. The first quart of water I drank, I immediately hurled right back out. It took a while to hold anything down but I was soon drinking and showering myself with all the water I could handle. I ate some food and slept for a few hours.

It took me hours to recuperate, to even stand up, but I awoke feeling like a new man. The whole thing seemed like some bizarre dream. I walked back to my line and rappelled. I cleaned my gear and was soon standing on the summit again with an official time of 51 hours and 14 minutes. Not exactly a speed climb, but that didn't matter to me anymore. Two years later, I found the phantom water bottle on Plastic Surgery Disaster.

Don't underestimate how hot it can get and how much water you can actually go through. That was the main lesson. And I learned that it's a lot easier climbing with a partner. When I climbed Eagle's Way again with my buddy Brian McCray, we were back down on the ground celebrating with a beer before the sun went down. That felt a lot better though soloing can be rewarding as well.

I gathered up my gear with a big smile. I felt more alive than I'd ever felt in my life. I'll be ticking off El Cap routes until I take the big dirt nap, but I knew this was one adventure that I'd never forget. It rose above everything else I'd ever done. I started down the East Ledges with a joyful skip in my stride.

Richard Leversee and John Wason: "The Nature of an Epic"

As much as rock climbing thrives in Yosemite, little ice climbing occurs there for two main reasons. First, the park seldom experiences weather cold enough to freeze its famed waterfalls. Second, the pursuit appeals only to a small number of alpinists willing to brave loose ice, below-freezing temperatures and hypothermia. Yet these hardy climbers experience a face of Yosemite few will ever see.

That was the goal of three who attempted the 2,000-foot Widow's Tears ice climb in January of 2002. Their team did not want for experience. Richard Leversee, then 43, had achieved the first ascent of The Dream Stream ice climb on Lower Sentinel Falls. John Wason, 42, had scaled Half Dome in a day and ascended a dozen routes on El Capitan. And Dan McDevitt, 42, climbed and guided in the park for decades, achieving more than 100 first ascents. The trio waited years to plant their axes and crampons onto the highest ice climb in the lower 48 states, which tested them like never before.

RL: Yosemite Valley ice climbs have always been an elusive quarry at best. I had an arrangement with Dan and his wife Sue who worked in the valley. They would keep an eye on Widow's Tears and call if it got anywhere near climbable. More often I would call to bug them to look if I knew the temperatures were getting close.

JW: Richard had been calling me for a week, telling me that the weather was very cold and ice was starting to form. With each call he got progressively more excited, leaving messages like, "We have reached DEFCON 3; be prepared to pack at a moment's notice."

RL: For years I had wanted to climb it. The formation is rare and doesn't form every year. The ice requires many straight days of very cold weather with no warm spikes. You have to wait, watch and be ready to drop everything at a moment's notice to go when it's ready. I love that game. Besides, I love suffering for suffering's sake and ice climbing is a good sport for that.

JW: We met in El Portal at Dan's house around 11 p.m. We got up early and left the car at 4:30 a.m. for the approach. After two hours of bushwhacking up through a snowy field of scree, we arrived at the base. Richard was jumping off the ground with each step in excitement. He had worked himself into a frenzy. We were really psyched as it began to get light and we dumped our ski poles and put on crampons.

Up we went, through the two rope lengths to the top of the third class section. Easy climbing, but two of us had packs with cameras, extra clothes, an extra rack and such. The next part was a 400-foot snowfield with poor snow conditions. It took more time than we wanted to get to the first pitch.

RL: It's most rare to get enough ice to cover the lower slabs. Without that it's like torture because you can see the beautiful upper pitches but you can't reach them. On this particular day the bottom ice was thin and ghostly gray but climbable.

JW: Richard took the first pitch, using ice screws and a bit of rock gear. A 60-meter pitch barely got him to the top of the first step, well below where we thought. Why is it that big ice climbs look small at the base until you start to climb them? It seemed unreal. Dan led the next pitch, a short one with cool climbing to a rock anchor.

RL: John's a rope gun, just an animal on ice. He led both the crux pitches. The upper ice was nice and thick. We kept the belay stations to the side of the climbing route to avoid falling shrapnel.

JW: The harder climbing was very interesting and the pitch took

Widow's Tears   Photo: Richard Leversee

an unexpected line up the steeper section to stay on the sticky ice. The protection was good and the ice got thicker the higher I climbed. By the anchor, the ice was running with water. I had to squeeze out my gloves twice.

RL: One challenging thing about climbing Widow's Tears is that even when it's cold enough to form, the temperature warms throughout the day and you get water coming down the ice. Everything you wear gets soaked to the bone. We knew that and brought three pairs of gloves each. Even so, all our gloves were soaked before the end of the day.

JW: Belaying up my partners became a challenge at this point. The ropes were completely soaked, very heavy and barely able to fit through a belay device. The hardest thing was just lifting the ropes up. I was completely worked from the belaying by the time they got to me.

RL: The climb gets really hairy when water inevitably soaks the rope, even if it's waterproof, on the second half of the day. Then when temperatures drop, the rope freezes and becomes a steel cable. We eventually had to forget the belay devices and switch to hip belays.

JW: Richard took the next pitch and methodically made his way up. Dan and I followed. A peregrine falcon, our brother in flight, swooped by us and called. An uneventful pitch turned epic as I reached the belay. My hands, completely soaked for two pitches, were frozen and began to thaw. I was brought to my knees and cried out loud. After several minutes, I regained my composure.

My next pitch turned out to be longer and steeper than it looked. A full 60 meters took me to thick ice and a small ledge. Then the real work began. I tried to belay while running the ropes through the anchor. I needed two hands just to pull the ropes, coated in ice and very heavy. At that point I was really scared about my ability to stop a fall. Belaying this pitch was the absolute crux for me.

RL: The next pitch I led was still pretty steep, but the critical issue was time. The sun was setting and we were all very aware of the dropping temperatures and what was happening with the rope. We had to climb without stopping to prevent the rope from freezing to the ice. If you're stuck to the ice with a frozen rope and no bivvy gear after sundown, you're done. You will die. And even if you did somehow survive the night, the rope will be even more frozen on the next day.

So when it came time to remove an ice screw or anchor a belay, we had to do it really quickly to keep the rope moving. When I belayed the others up the pitch, I brought them both at the same time on one rope to speed things up and sent them past me without stopping.

JW: We scrambled up the last 100 feet to the summit. I clipped off to a tree and turned out my light. The sky was liquid black, stars shimmering everywhere. I could hear the sound of the wind in the tall fir trees. Relief poured into my veins. This was a good climb. We celebrated with some energy bars and water as temperatures dropped quickly to the low teens or single digits.

RL: At the top of climb the rope was so frozen that we couldn't untie the knots in our harnesses. We cut ourselves loose with a knife. I was sorely tempted to leave the rope behind because it weighed so much.

The descent was exhausting. We had to posthole[1] through miles of thigh-deep snow. We would go for a 100 yards or so, collapse and rest. We would actually sleep a few seconds or maybe a minute. Then the cold would wake us and we'd move again, chilled to the bone. Walk, drop, sleep, freeze, repeat. We did that for hours, steering by intuition. For an extra little challenge, our headlamps died.

JW: We got back to the car at 1:30 a.m., jumped in and drove back

---

1. posthole: to trudge through deep snow

to Dan's house. Dan and I went inside and woke Sue to join the party. We cracked beers, started a fire and heated some soup on the stove. Then we asked, "Where's Richard?"

RL: The heater in my van didn't work very well. We were back at Dan's house before it started to warm up. I couldn't pull myself away from it when they went inside. I took off all my wet clothes and slowly started to get dry and warm. We had been wet all day. When you sweat on a lead climb and then stop to belay and become stationary in sub-freezing temperatures, it's a recipe for hypothermia. That was the coldest I've ever been.

JW: Dan urged him in to no avail. After a bit, Sue went out and came back saying, "I'm not sure what's going on, but Richard is butt naked in his van!" Eventually Richard came in, thawed out and we all drank a toast to good friends and good climbing. We stumbled to bed around 4 a.m.

RL: There's something about the nature of an epic. When things get that serious and that hard, life is really real. Earlier in my life, I was motivated by the lust and passion of elusive climbs. I was willing to do pretty much anything to climb them. I'm not that motivated now. I don't ever want to be that cold again.

  Widow's Tears is definitely the greatest adventure I've ever been on. I never want to go back. There's an interesting dynamic of how that works. Some of the most memorable experiences in life are ones we would never wish to repeat.

Andy Padlo:
"Summit Fever"

*Yosemite's world-class granite walls attract the majority of climbers'
attention and efforts, though dozens of worthy mountaineering challenges
fill the park's backcountry. While parties wait in line to get on popular Yosemite Valley rock climbs, those who trek long distances to attempt high
country peaks usually find themselves alone.*

*Andy Padlo has been known to take the path less traveled. A member of
the Pinecrest Nordic Ski Patrol and a backpacking guide, Padlo has hiked
through the nearby Emigrant Wilderness more than the area's own rangers.
His cycling résumé includes a coast-to-coast journey, multiple mountain
pass crossings and a trip from San Francisco to Yosemite and back that
traced the footsteps of John Muir. On three separate occasions starting in
2002, the summit of 13,120-foot Mount Lyell eluded him. True to form, he
decided to make his next effort more unique and challenging by attempting
the park's highest mountain in winter conditions during May of 2006.*

Backcountry mountaineering offers anyone who loves climbing and backpacking the extra appeal of multiple challenges
that test one's skill, character and decision making. Instead
of following a trail, the mountaineer uses his map, compass, experience and even intuition to make his way. The terrain presents many
problems and obstacles that engage the whole mind and body of the
outdoorsman. The experience can also be likened to the childhood
pleasure one got in climbing rocks and trees, scrambling up and over
precipices and so forth. This pure joy and sense of adventure resur-
faces in the heart and eyes of the mountain trekker.

I can't speak for everyone who goes out to climb in the mountains, but I begin to take certain mountaineering goals and challenges personally. If a particular peak or climb seems within my ability, or a bit beyond, I am not satisfied until I've made it to the top or across the distance. It seems more than just a personal goal I've set for myself. It takes on a personality of its own and seems to wait there for me almost like a friend to whom I've promised something. The time I spend in the mountains fills my thinking much of the time when I am home in the city. I can almost say there is some sense of personal identity I feel with the whole experience of hiking, climbing and camping in the high wilderness areas. Hence, a failure to reach a certain goal can become a sort of obsession with unfinished personal business.

I'd been turned around on Lyell before. My old friend Reid Russell and I went out once to climb it in October 2002. However, we didn't take ice axes or crampons, so we weren't sure we could negotiate the frozen glacier. Anyhow, we took longer than we thought we would hiking into Emerald Lake, and settled for taking a picture of Lyell from the north. I placed the picture on the wall of my cabin. That's what got me thinking about taking a more serious approach to climbing the mountain.

I was intrigued enough to join a group of my cousins and friends on an October climb a few years later. I watched, plagued with foot pain, from the southern saddle just below the peak while two of our party scrambled to the summit. My boots were tight and had worn giant blisters on both feet. We'd climbed the boiler-plate ice of the glacier as a party of six using ice axes and crampons but fourth- and fifth-class rock climbing made up the final approach. I hadn't done much technical climbing then and wasn't too confident in my skills on spent legs. My cousin Matt Johanson and our friend Cliff DeYoung, experienced climbers both, advised against the rest of us following them on the southern ridge to the summit. They had to make a few exposed moves to gain the top, and perhaps they were right. It was best to save my climb for another day. Since I'd gotten so close, I felt compelled to go back. From then on a photo of Mt. Lyell appeared as desktop wallpaper on my computer.

The next early spring, I packed my skis into my car and drove six hours from San Francisco to June Lake, parked and set off to summit Lyell alone. I made it to Donohue Pass the evening of my second day out. From there I ventured forward only to hear the tell-tale "whumps" of loose snow slabs for hundreds of yards around me. When you hear that, you know the snow conditions are too dangerous to continue. So I regretfully turned back down Rush Creek Canyon, camped and skied out the next day. I happened to break my sunglasses on a fall that last morning and suffered a bit of snow blindness that slowed my drive home. My eyes seemed to fill with sand, the pain grew worse and my vision blurred. I drove in five- and ten-minute increments. All in all, it took me 18 hours to drive back to San Francisco.

So of course I went out again the next year to try again. I drove to Silver Lake alone in May, planning to ski up Rush Creek Trail and over Donohue Pass. This time Cliff and his father Richard DeYoung planned to join me. They would ski up from the valley, through Tuolumne and down Lyell Canyon to meet me at the Lyell headwaters. From there we planned to climb Mt. Lyell together.

At the Silver Lake parking lot I noticed a creek and break in the wall of cliffs that seemed to offer a faster way up and into the Rush Creek drainage. I hiked up through the willows to snow level and skied from there into a small bowl south of Mt. Wood. I met a local skier there and asked him if I could get to "the lakes" by continuing up this narrow canyon. He assured me I could. Trouble was, later I realized he'd meant Alger Lakes, not the ones I had in mind, Agnew and Waugh. Too tired to take a look at the map, I climbed a steep snow-filled ravine alongside a cascading spring creek that plunged now and then back into the snow field. By evening I'd reached a small crescent moon of a valley where the skier had told me he'd just destroyed his snow cave. I found the remains of the burrow, pitched my bottomless tent and went to sleep after a cold snack.

I checked the map in the morning and realized I was north of my intended route, but felt the drainage I saw heading west of Alger Lakes would bring me to a way up and over the crest ahead. I've always been an improviser in my backcountry trips. To find a new route sounded fun and exciting! My park service map was not of the highest resolution, but there seemed to be a couple of fairly moderate slopes I could get down once I'd gotten over Blacktop Mountain.

The morning was bright and warm. I had an exhilarating climb over wide and empty snow fields up to the final climb of the Kuna Crest, north of Donahue Pass. A little past noon I reached the broad pebbly plateau atop Blacktop Mountain. I dropped my gear and scouted around for a way down into Lyell Canyon. I found nothing but sheer drops and scary steep couloirs. A better mountaineer than I could maybe ski one of these chutes, but I'd run up against the limits of my ability to "make it work somehow." I sat and ate lunch, settling in to the depressing fact that I'd have to ski all the way back down the way I'd come. Then I'd have to go back up another route fast enough to catch Cliff and Richard.

Before setting off back down the canyon, I decided to take a walk further south down the ridge to have one last look, just in case. I happened to spy a narrow, snow-filled gully that didn't seem too terrifyingly steep. There were rocks exposed on one side which offered a way to climb down without having to risk getting out on the ice and snow. I strapped my skis to my pack, removed my crampons, and stepped gingerly in my plastic boots downward into the gully. I soon found the rocks slick with ice and the steepness uncomfortable as I struggled downward, slipping now and then. With my hands on loose rock holds and face to the mountain, I lowered myself one footstep at a time.

My heavy pack swayed on my shoulders because of the skis. I decided to try the snow instead. The angle was still too steep for my comfort as a skier, and the rocks that jutted out here and there made a fall too dangerous, so I stabilized myself on a platform of a rock. I put on my crampons, took out my ice axe and traversed out onto the snow, front pointing my way downward. After each kick, I lowered my ice axe point to anchor it at about chest level, then kicked in lower steps again, over and over.

Each time I shifted my weight, however, I felt my pack pulling me backwards, threatening to yank me from my anchor. I didn't know how long I was going to be out there and had packed way too much stuff. I took a sling, tied it around my waist, then carefully took off my pack and clipped it to the sling so that the pack and skis dangled below me between my legs on the snow. This felt much more bal-

Donahue Pass

Photo: Cliff DeYoung

anced and secure, but after another 20 yards or so, I began to feel the same dangerous pull of all my gear trying to tear me from my hold on the slope. I was already tired and with 1,000 feet more to descend, I began to resent and even hate my own pack!

Without thinking much about it, I reached down with one hand, pulled my skis from the side straps of my pack, aimed them straight down the couloirs and let them go. They hissed at amazing speed downward, caught their tips, and cartwheeled over and over towards the bottom of the ridge. They came to rest far out on the shelf below, one ski sticking straight up out of the snow. I then handled the carabineer in the sling, unclipped it, and without another thought let my pack go as well. It slid for a while, gathered speed, hit a bump and bounced into the air with such fury I felt a bit afraid. Then it spun end over end, spewing my cook pot, food and other gear as it crashed on down the slope.

I was free now to work my way downward. After a while longer I was able to turn and plunge my heels into the softer snow of the lower slope, gather up my gear and put back on my skis, which were thankfully unbroken. I had a sheepish feeling that someone must be looking out for me after I got away with such careless treatment of my equipment. I continued on my way west toward Donahue Pass.

I skied down into the Lyell Headwaters at dusk, called out for Cliff and Richard and blew my whistle into the gathering darkness. There was no answer. I then felt sure I'd missed them somehow and that I'd be climbing Lyell alone. I figured it couldn't be any worse than what I'd just done. I dug in under a large boulder to pitch my tent and collapse.

But the next morning, I noticed ski tracks right next to my tent. I hurried to put together some food and gear and then chased out into the morning. I climbed following the tracks and soon heard Cliff and Richard joyously responding to my shouts. We quickly traded stories, put our stuff together and set out for Lyell.

I dropped my skis, put on crampons and set off straight up the glacier that reached almost to the summit. At a certain point, the steepness of the slope and the sketchy nature of the ice had me struggling to hang on to the mountain and avoid sliding all the way back down onto the glacier face. My crampon tips held, however. Neither

Cliff nor Richard had crampons or ice axes. They were not comfortable climbing the last steep section of the peak in their skis. So they made the climb on the exposed rocks north of the summit. We all made it to the top in good time.

Our spirits were high, but I began to notice my own exhaustion at this point. On the ski back down I had to stop several times and rub the cramps out of my burning thighs. Cliff and Richard went over Donohue Pass and I was supposed to break down my camp and follow them. But I was so tired when I reached my tent that I lay down to rest and fell fast asleep. Hours later I shot up out of my nap and realized the guys must be worried about me. I packed up quickly, climbed up over Donohue Pass, and met Cliff on his way back down, looking for me. We camped a mile or so down from the pass as my legs began to give out on me again.

Our next day was a long slow negotiation of mixed snow and rock, with some debate about the best route out to Silver Lake. We finally decided to simply follow the route of the summer trail out through Agnew Lake. As dusk approached we had about two miles to go to the car. We had the long traverse of the reservoir across a steep snowfield left to do, and again we were facing mixed conditions. Since we had to take off our skis to walk the rocky sections, we finally opted for keeping them off even in the snow and ice. This turned out to be a mistake for Cliff and Richard who had no ice axes for self arrest in case of a slip.

On a particularly treacherous stretch of ice covered with a layer of softened snow, Richard lost his balance and slid downward until his leg suddenly caught in the snow. The momentum drove his foot down under him while his upper body fell forward under the weight of his pack, twisting his knee almost entirely around. He came to rest on exposed rocks at the edge of a small cliff. Tough guy that he is, he immediately tried to stand on the bad leg, howled in pain and collapsed. Cliff and I came to our senses and made our way down to help. Richard eventually was able to walk out slowly the last two miles, leaning on a ski pole, carefully holding his leg in such a position that the damaged ligament would not give way. At the truck, we packed his knee in ice, and drove home in good spirits.

It's a great route. I would take some protection on that down

Andy Padlo (center) and companions at Mt. Lyell   Photo: Cliff DeYoung

climb next time, although now I feel I'm a better skier and could maybe get down on my skis. Moments climbing down that chute were immensely terrifying, and yet it was greatly satisfying to overcome that fear, get down and then look back up and say I did that. It was really fun finding a route that was pretty much untraveled. I did not have any trail book or guide book description giving me a sense of safety. This is what I find immensely gratifying in trips like this: problem solving and attaining a goal, depending entirely on my ability to read a map and negotiate difficult routes.

After this trip I decided I needed to work more on specific mountaineering skills, such as descending steep slopes on skis rather than trying to down-climb them. I found a real love for winter travel. The isolation, the challenge of route-finding and the extreme conditions make for a true test of skill and wits. I also realized the need to take very seriously the chances of mishap or accident. I began to get trained in wilderness medicine and to work with the Pinecrest Nordic Ski Patrol as a way to build my knowledge and abilities in winter mountaineering.

Overall, I didn't learn so much from this adventure as I gained in a sense of accomplishment and peace. For whatever reason I'd been a victim of summit fever, and the ultimate success of this four-day trip — getting into Lyell Canyon, finding my friends, reaching the peak, and getting back in one piece — led to a new emphasis. I began looking to bring others out into the Sierras, to organize trips for students and to show them the mountains. I don't feel like I need to go out and do every extreme trek or climb out there, but instead I feel like I know the mountains well enough now to guide others out to have adventures of their own.

Tommy Caldwell:
"That Old-School Style"

Reaching the top is no longer enough. As climbers defeat ever more obstacles once thought impossible, stars of the sport set their sights on climbing those routes faster, with less gear or in better style. For instance, ascending a big wall in a single push trumps a prolonged, up-and-down siege.

By the age of 28, Tommy Caldwell had joined the small fraternity of elite climbers who observe these distinctions to test themselves. His résumé already boasted eight free ascents on El Capitan including first free ascents of West Buttress and Dihedral Wall. Seeking a worthy project, Caldwell and longtime partner Beth Rodden attempted The Captain's notorious El Corazon (5.13b) in May of 2007. Scaling its 35 pitches totally without aid or previous route experience would have abundantly challenged anyone. Because an outdated topo map led them to climb without a hammer or pitons, Caldwell and Rodden faced the added terror of long unprotected pitches with potential for wild pendulum falls.

A bead of sweat ran down my forehead. I blinked rapidly and tears ran down my cheek. Was I crying or sweating? Considering where I was, probably both. A couple of feet below my position on The Bunny Slope pitch of El Corazon was a large roof and then 2,000 feet of air to El Cap's base. In the last 60 feet of free climbing there were only two pieces of gear. One of them was an upside-down stopper slotted between two face holds. A crack was just inches away but I had been stuck in the same spot for more than an hour, too chicken to commit to the tenuous, irreversible 5.13 moves to reach it.

These days when most people want to free climb El Capitan, they walk around to the top, rappel down and top-rope their route so they can work out the moves. Then once they've got it down, they come around and start over from the bottom. Ten years ago there were only a few people who free climbed El Cap, but now it's exploded in terms of free climbing popularity and that's the reason. The style has evolved and climbers have figured out that it's easier to do it this way.

I wanted a bigger challenge and a taste of the climbing style that people did back in the old days. So on El Corazon, I decided to start at the bottom and not pre-rehearse any of it. The route is infamous for being run out and scary. If you've come down from the top and figured out the pitches first, it's not so bad to do scary stuff because you know what you're getting into. But it's much harder when you start free climbing at the bottom, not knowing much about the route, not knowing where the protection goes and facing big fall potential. Alex Huber put up the route a few years earlier but the only information I had about it came from a topo map and a little blurb in a climbing magazine.

We climbed the bottom half of the route smoothly in a day. There was supposed to be a scary pitch above the Gray Ledges. You're supposed to do this big dynamic lunge 40 feet above a ledge with one shallow piton as the only protection. I was really worried about that but I found some rivets on a route to the left. We went that way and I was able to equalize a couple of them to protect the pitch. I'm not generally into dangerous climbing. I like to push myself physically but I don't want to die up there. I've climbed a lot of dangerous things and I'm always analyzing and really calculating how to make them as safe as possible.

Next are these four pitches of very long traverses in a row. These turned out to be really epic. I was willing to risk huge falls on these run out traverses but I wasn't about to have Beth do the same. So we devised a super-involved plan that, though labor intensive and extremely time consuming, would keep the second safe. As I climbed each pitch, I also set a haul line which she could use to protect her traverse while I belayed her on a top rope. Then I had to rappel the route to clean the anchor and gear and finally follow it again. There

El Corazon on El Capitan

might be a better way to do it but I couldn't figure one out at the time. These complicated logistics meant that each of the traversing pitches took half a day. At this pace we would top out in about three weeks. We brought food and water for only five days.

Then we got to a 5.12d pitch, which I knew Leo Houlding had tried a few years earlier. He's known for being a super bold climber but he got turned around and I never found out why. When Huber did it, there had been a bunch of fixed pitons on the route. The topo map showed them too. But there were none when I got there. Someone had cleaned them all out and I didn't have a hammer or any pitons with me.

So I had to climb up this thing, real scared on bad pro and almost falling on several occasions. It would have been a terrible fall. I started thinking I was going to have to bail, though it would be really hard to reverse the pitches we'd done and I wasn't sure we even could. Over to the right I saw more rivets. I ended up climbing this big overhanging off-width crack, without any big gear, to reach the rivets and clip into them. I managed to get around to the top of this pitch and find an anchor so I could set up a top rope. This took about half a day.

Finally we got that pitch done, and then the next pitch was called The Bunny Slope. We were barely halfway up the route at this point and we only had a day's worth of food and water left. Again the topo map showed these small bird beak pitons. There were supposed to be a few of these fixed on the pitch, but there weren't. My only protection was the belay, around the corner where I couldn't even see, and it was 5.12c, super-slick slab climbing. I spent two hours climbing back and forth as my calves got pumped trying to get brave enough to go on. How do I do this?

Eventually I figured out how to climb to a horizontal slot. I was able to put an upside-down nut in it. This gave me a little confidence. I was going a completely different way than the first ascent because those pitons were just not there. I could see on my left a groove where it looked like there was a crack. I figured if I could traverse and make a couple of hard moves over to it, I'd be able to put in gear and then I'd be fine. But I was looking at a 60-foot fall, if my crappy placements held, that would leave me spinning 2,000 feet in space and probably yank Beth through the belay. I looked back at the upside-down nut, tried to imagine it was closer and better than it actually was, tried to psych myself up to commit to the 5.13 sequence … and then hesitated for another 45 minutes. Beth was around the corner wondering what the heck is going on because usually I'm a pretty fast climber. This was getting ridiculous.

Finally I committed to this move, I did the traverse and discovered there was no crack. There was just a really thin groove and no place for gear. I just had to turn it on and get into this total free solo mode to climb up this virtually unprotected 5.12 corner.

The whole time I was trying to convince myself that if I fell, it would be okay. There was a big roof below me and even if my piece failed, even if I took a huge 100-foot swing, it would be a clean fall. One nice thing about El Cap is that it's so sheer, there's not a lot to hit on a fall. You can get away with taking huge ones. A few years earlier when I was speed climbing Lurking Fear, I took a 120-foot, head-first fall that was pretty scary but didn't hurt me. I've heard stories of people taking 200- or even 300-foot falls. El Cap is one of the only places I know where you can do that. But it's hard to convince yourself that's the case and it becomes this mental game.

Luckily I pulled off the moves and fixed the rope. Beth followed on top rope and she did just fine. Above that, we followed these good cracks the rest of the way. We had 11 pitches left and a couple of them were 5.13, but we sped up to finish and topped out in a day.

To climb in that old-school style is definitely a lot harder and more adventurous so it's cool to do occasionally. On this one, I walked away thinking, "Man, that was stressful and dangerous." I'm not sure it was worth it. A lot of climbers are all about the danger and the fear. I feel like it's selfish to be excessively dangerous. This time I probably pushed it a little farther than I should have. The climb forced me to be really creative. I was always thinking about ways to solve problems that were not simple and which I'd never encountered before, even after climbing on El Cap for eight years by that point.

Not bringing a hammer was really a mistake. I just figured that it was an existing route and I wouldn't need one. Climbers are usually pretty poor which is why they often remove their own pitons. And if they come across other pitons, they sometimes take those as booty. I think that's what happened there. So I learned I should probably bring a hammer and a few pitons on routes that I don't know anything about in case the topo map is wrong.

After I freed El Cap twice in a day, I said that it felt like a crag to me. This didn't feel anything like a crag. I felt intimidated and strung out. But then again, I had asked for this. In some remote corner of my mind I craved this kind of adventure. I wanted and needed to be pushed hard. What made me think I could do the most notoriously scary free route on El Cap this way? I guess it was ego. It's great to be humbled by the big walls and by the mountains as I try harder and harder climbs. It makes you careful and builds character. This was one of those experiences for me.

Yosemite Falls

Afterword

We shivered all night beneath a starry sky and threw rocks at wild mice which threatened our meager food supply. Until you've toughed out a night on a rocky ledge at 6,000 feet without sleeping bags or jackets, you just haven't lived.

Early in my climbing career, two friends and I attempted Braille Book, a moderate six-pitch route on Higher Cathedral Rock. Wary of the August heat, we set out around noon to climb in shade. Our late start shielded us from the sun, but it also left us trapped on a small and slanted outcropping after dark, completely unequipped to bivouac. Sleepy and cold, we summited near dawn, descended to the valley and demolished a massive breakfast at Curry Village.

The debacle caused us to laugh at ourselves and made a good story to tell, though compared to other Yosemite epics, ours was a pebble at the base of El Capitan. I enjoyed hearing many more dramatic tales around campfires over the years. In the process, I realized that smoothly-completed climbs, ski treks and other outings make for great fun and memories. The most enjoyable stories, however, feature some suspense, unexpected challenges, lessons learned and happy endings.

Those are the elements I sought in tales for this book, first from outdoors folks I knew from Yosemite and later from others I met through my research. Inspired by the fine first-person narratives produced by such writers as Studs Terkel and Lawrence Ritter, I strove to capture accounts of epics in the words of the people involved. Most of this book's contributors generously offered me their time for interviews and assistance in proofreading these stories. Some went even further and wrote their own epic tales which I edited only lightly. Because many outstanding writers have documented Yosemite's fascinating history in other works, I looked for episodes which have attracted little or no previous attention.

As a result of these criteria, this book by no means represents a definitive collection of epic Yosemite adventures. Readers seeking broader examinations of this subject will enjoy "Camp 4: Recollections of a Yosemite Rockclimber" by Steve Roper, "The Vertical World of Yosemite" by Galen Rowell and "The Wild Muir: Twenty-two of John Muir's Greatest Adventures," by Lee Stetson. Each of these books inspired and educated me. In producing "Yosemite Epics," I aimed to add some fresh voices and light-hearted memories to the park's collective literature. I'm thrilled to preserve and share new recollections from both well-known and lesser-known mountaineers which I, at least, found exciting, instructive and fun.

An unexpected and heartbreaking event put a twist into my thinking, however. World-renowned climber John Bachar provided one of my first interviews in June of 2009. He kindly shared the story of his close call while free soloing on The Moratorium, largely defending the practice of climbing without rope despite its tremendous danger. Two weeks later I was crushed to learn he died after falling on an unroped climb near his Eastern Sierra home.

Bachar's story seemed to fit perfectly into my desired format when I first heard it. But following his tragic death, I pondered long whether to include it in this volume. Though I believe all outdoors enthusiasts accept some risk in their activities, the hazards he embraced seem to me both unnecessary and reckless. Yet he didn't see it that way, even after his narrow escape from The Moratorium and other scares. Could I do right by him without betraying the premise of the book?

Ultimately I decided to include his tale but not to make a statement for or against free soloing. Rather, I hope its inclusion helps to drive home a broader and more critical point. All the activities described in these pages are inherently dangerous, sometimes more so than even the participants recognized, and Bachar wasn't the only one who took a different lesson from his epic than I would have. I

John Bachar in June of 2009

believe the stories within make the case for expanding one's limits slowly, exercising every precaution and erring on the side of safety. This collection purposefully focuses on tales that end well, but no one should draw false or rosy conclusions from these hand-chosen episodes. Other works such as "Off the Wall: Death in Yosemite" and the annual "Accidents in North American Mountaineering" extensively document the risks that accompany outdoors adventure. Epics cease to amuse when people get badly hurt or worse.

I didn't get to know Bachar well but I did discover that he was far more than a climber who liked to live on the edge. In our hour together, he was warm, friendly, considerate and helpful. Later I learned that he was a devoted father and a dear friend to many. Had John lived longer, I would have followed up with him on his evolving thoughts about free soloing. He did not encourage others to emulate him in our interview and actively discouraged climbers from doing so in other published statements. Clearly Bachar had at least one thing in common with people likely to read these words: he loved Yosemite and the outdoors.

So do I, which is why I keep returning year after year. While I discover something new each time, I still feel I've only scratched the surface. Most of my outings are enjoyable but uneventful, which suits me fine. I don't have a story that compares with those in the book. There was one ski trek, though, which felt epic at the time.

On our first trip to Ostrander Hut, a group of friends and I made every dumb mistake in the book. First we started late on one of the shortest days of the year. Then we rented flimsy skis ill-suited to the black diamond terrain. Finally, we carried little bivvy gear which was woefully inadequate for our inevitable night out in the snow. After we dug in as best we could, I discovered that the only stove I'd brought was out of fuel. The freezing night seemed to last forever. We retreated the next morning and never reached the hut that year.

All in all, it was a miserable experience and no way to impress my new girlfriend Karen. But she married me anyway. See, the happy ending makes the story, doesn't it?

Acknowledgments

C reating this book often felt like climbing a mountain: challenging, daunting, sometimes overwhelming yet profoundly rewarding. I'm grateful to an exceptional summit team which helped me reach the top.

For supporting and encouraging my writing over the years, thanks to Angela Bass, Sorana Bucur, Anne Chalfant, Cathy Claesson, Buzz Eggleston, Bob Evans, Frank-Deiter Freiling, Pete Gauvin, Jeff Gire, Kristina Hacker, Joel Harris, Sean Harvey, Mario Scherhaufer, Mark Slider, Ann Tatko-Peterson, Mark Trautwein, Greg Watkins and the International Center for Journalists.

Producing the book was truly a group effort. Helpful advice and guidance came from Steve Babuljak, Serena Bartlett, Susie Bennitt, Glen Denny, Hans Florine, Cheryl Koehler, Bob Lorentzen, Chris McNamara, John Moynier, Barry Parr and Suzanne Swedo.

For assistance in proofreading, extra credit goes to Bianca Arias, Anna Balassone, Matt Barney, Nic Barradas, Natalie Chin, SangEun Choi, Daniel Chung, Abby Clark, Kearny Combs, Rebecca Fong, Dan Galvan, Reyna Garcia, Sarah Gilchriese, Lawrence Ham, Alicia Harger, Jason Hazari, Yoon Jung, Max Kahane, Simrit Kaur, Erin Kim, Kate Kim, Trevor Kwong, Dana Lin, Emily Lin-Jones, John London, Tim Pak, Holden Parks, Jennifer Price, Andie Smith and Hillman Zheng.

Thanks to designer and photo editor Morry Angell, copy editors Bill Gracie and Ben Topkins, photographers Cliff DeYoung and Dan Johanson and web site designer Jeff Stevens. I'm especially grateful to artist Christopher Hampson, who threw his great talent behind this project early on and labored for more than a year on its fine illustrations.

I offer warm thanks to the Yosemite pioneers and enthusiasts who kindly shared the stories within these pages. I'd never met most of them prior to our interviews. Getting to know these great people was a privilege and a highlight of the project. I'm equally grateful to those who shared tales which could not fit into the book's limited space. Special thanks to Errett Allen, Majka Burhardt, George Durkee, Peter Mayfield, Marty McDonnell, Ammon McNeely, Andy Padlo and John Wason who wrote their own "epics."

Finally, I'm lucky to have close friends and family members who spend time with me outdoors in Yosemite and elsewhere. Our countless enjoyable and sometimes character-building adventures inspired this book. Heartfelt thanks to Morry Angell, Bill Bailey, Paul Denzler, Cliff DeYoung, Richard DeYoung, Keith Doran, Randall Dunn, John Dunphy, Bob Leung, Dan Johanson, Karen Johanson, Steve Johanson, Ted Johanson, Tom and Diane Johanson, Linnae Johansson, Peter Johansson, Raffi Kevorkian, Allan MacKenzie, Andy Padlo, Anna Padlo, Lynn Padlo, Zach Padlo and Tim Wyman. I'm also looking forward to many future outings with my young nephews Tommy Johanson and Nathan Johanson.

– Matt Johanson

I would like to thank my mother for sacrificing and working hard to raise me and my brothers well. Thanks also to Matt Harding, an honest and helpful critic, and Ed and Lily Noon, whose support has been invaluable. Most of all I thank my wife Joanna Hampson, who puts up with me being an artist.

– Christopher Hampson

Explanation of Climbing Ratings

Climbers in Yosemite and elsewhere use ratings systems to define and describe terrain. They start by classifying the difference between flat ground, the vertical world and everything in between:

Class 1: easy walking
Class 2: simple scrambling on hilly or rough territory
Class 3: heavier scrambling on steep ground using handholds and footholds
Class 4: simple climbing on steeper and harder terrain with dangerous fall potential
Class 5: climbing requiring gear, ropes and belays for protection

Class 5 free climbs are rated with a second number that indicates their difficulty. Climbs rated from 5.0 to 5.6 are suitable for beginners. Routes from 5.7 to 5.9 are intermediate. Only experts should attempt climbs 5.10 and higher. Routes in this range are further distinguished with letters a, b, c and d. For example, 5.14d is harder climbing than 5.14a. This is known as the Yosemite Decimal System, which climbers also use outside the park and throughout the United States.

Aid climbs require the use of gear to assist in upward progress, as opposed to merely for protection against falling. The hardest routes are possibly only as aid climbs, although free climbers constantly push the boundaries of what they can do without aid. Aid ratings begin at A0 for the easiest climbs and top out at A5 for the most difficult and dangerous routes.

As many climbers scale routes using a mixture of free and aid climbing techniques, some climbs in this book have multiple ratings (for example, The Nose, 5.13b/A2). These figures indicate the maximum difficulty of climbing the entire routes in each of the disciplines.

Glossary

aid (n): climbing gear used to assist in upward progress

aid, aid climb (v): to climb while using gear to assist in upward progress, instead of only to protect against falls

alpenstock: a strong hiking staff with a sharp point

anchor: a secure gear arrangement on a climb used to protect belay stations

aréte: a sharp rock edge or ridge

ascenders: metal tools used to grip and ascend climbing ropes, sometimes called Jumars

back-cleaning: to remove gear beneath a climber before establishing a secure anchor, greatly increasing the risk of a catastrophic fall

BASE jumping: skydiving without a plane from a high point like a mountain peak; BASE stands for building, antenna, span or earth

An ascender

belay: to protect a climber from falling by securing the rope

beta: information about a climb

biner: see carabiner

bivouac, bivvy: to spend a night outdoors with little or no gear

bolt: a metal anchor placed in rock for climbing protection

cam: a spring-loaded climbing protection device that wedges into rock cracks

carabiner: metal ring with spring-loaded gates used to direct and secure rope

clean: to remove gear from a climb or to climb without placing bolts

A cam

chimney: a vertical shaft of rock

crag: a conveniently accessible climbing area

crampons: metal spikes that attach to boots to provide traction on ice and snow

crimp: to grip a small rock feature tenuously

crux: the most difficult part of a particular climb

Crampons

daisy chain: a sling with stiched loops used to secure a climber to aid gear

dihedral: a rock corner

epic: a dramatic outdoors event

figure eight knot: a common climbing knot used to tie one's harness to a rope

free, free climb: to climb using gear only to protect against falls, not to assist in upward progress

free solo: to climb alone and without rope or other protection

A figure eight knot

French free: to climb while pulling or stepping on gear

front point: to climb ice with crampons, using the front points to grip the ice

GPS: Global Positioning System, or any device using satellite technology to pinpoint location

jam: to wedge hands or feet into a crack in the process of climbing

jug, jugging: climbers' slang for ascending or jumaring up a rope

Jumars (n): metal tools used to grip and ascend climbing ropes; this proper name is often used generically; see ascenders

A hand jam

jumar (v): to use Jumars or ascenders to grip and ascend climbing ropes

lead (n): a climber's effort to ascend rock while placing protection

lead (v): to ascend rock while placing protection

leader: a climber who leads

lieback: a climbing technique using hands to pull on rock features while feet push simultaneously

mantle: a climbing move which involves pushing down with hands on a rock feature

nut: a climbing protection device with a metal piece attached to a wire which wedges into rock cracks

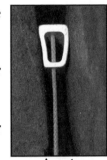

A nut

offwidth: a hard-to-grip rock crack which flares or lacks sharp edges

on sight: to climb a route one has never climbed or seen climbed before

overhang: a rock formation which forms an angle greater than 180 degrees in relation to the ground

pendulum: to swing on a rope, either in an awkward fall or deliberately to reach a location left or right of the climber

pig: climbers' slang for a haul bag

pitch: a unit of climbing distance usually up to one rope length long

piton: metal spike which climbers hammer into rock to provide protection or to build anchors

portaledge: a metal frame covered with fabric which provides climbers a flat refuge for resting or sleeping in vertical terrain

posthole: to trudge through deep snow

pro, protection: climbing gear used to protect against falls or to assist in upward progress

prusik (n): a knot used to grip and ascend rope

prusik (v): to use a prusik knot to grip and ascend rope

rappel (n): a descent on a secure rope

rap, rappel (v): to descend on a secure rope

rivet: a bolt lacking the usual hanger for placing carabiners, offering climbers only limited use for protection

runner: a sling used with carabiners to connect climbing protection to a rope

run out: a climbing effort with long spaces between gear placements, increasing the length of a potential fall

sandbag: a surprising difficult challenge

self arrest: to stop a fall on snow or ice using an ice axe

skins: fabrics which stick to ski bottoms to provide friction for climbing uphill

smear: a climbing technique using friction to hold feet on smooth or featureless rock

stem: to climb between two rock features using opposing pressure from hands or feet

stopper: a climbing protection device with a metal fragment attached to a wire; see nut

talus: a steep slope of rocks

traverse: to climb laterally

top rope: to climb with an anchor and rope already established above for protection wall: a long climb from the bottom to the top of a mountain face

whipper: a long or frightening fall

Bibliography

Anderson, Jay. "Climbing California's Mountains: Hikes, Scrambles and Nontechnical Climbs to the Summits." Guilford, Connecticut: Falcon, 2003.

Farabee, Charles and Ghiglieri, Michael. "Off the Wall: Death in Yosemite." Flagstaff, Arizona: Puma Press, 2007.

Florine, Hans and Wright, Bill. "Climb On! Skills for More Efficient Climbing." Guilford, Connecticut: Falcon, 2002.

Graydon, Don and Hanson, Kurt. "Mountaineering: The Freedom of the Hills." Seattle, Washington: Mountaineers, 1997.

McNamara, Chris. "Yosemite Valley Free Climbs." Mill Valley, California: Supertopo, 2003.

Reid, Don. "Yosemite Climbs: Big Walls." Evergreen, Colorado: Chockstone Press, 1993.

Reid, Don. "Yosemite Climbs: Free Climbs." Evergreen, Colorado: Chockstone Press, 1994.

Roper, Steve. "Camp 4: Recollections of a Yosemite Rockclimber." Seattle, Washington: Mountaineers, 1994.

Rowell, Galen. "The Vertical World of Yosemite: A Collection of Photographs and Writings on Rock Climbing in Yosemite." Berkeley, California: Wilderness Press, 1974.

Weamer, Howard. "The Perfect Art: Ostrander Hut and Ski Touring in Yosemite." Marceline, Montana: Walsworth Publishing, 1995.

Wilson, Herbert Earl. "The Lore and the Lure of the Yosemite: The Indians, Their Customs, Legends and Beliefs." San Francisco, California: Sunset Press, 1925.

About the Author

Matt Johanson writes about the outdoors, sports, education, travel and politics for California newspapers and magazines. "Yosemite Epics" is his third book. Prior works include "Game of My Life: San Francisco Giants." Matt also teaches social studies and advises an award-winning student newspaper at Castro Valley High School. He enjoys hiking, climbing and skiing in the Sierra Nevada mountains, especially Yosemite.

About the Illustrator

Christopher Hampson is an artist from Castro Valley, California who studied animation at the Academy of Art University in San Francisco. When not drawing like crazy he frequents Yosemite, Lake Tahoe and the local lakes for backpacking, snowboarding and mountain biking.